Friendship in Childhood and Adolescence

- Phil Erwin

LONDON AND NEW YORK

First published 1998
by Routledge
11 New Fetter Lane, London
EC4P 4EE

Simultaneously published in
the USA and Canada
by Routledge
29 West 35th Street, New York
NY 10001

© 1998 Phil Erwin

Typeset in Sabon and Futura by
Florencetype Ltd, Stoodleigh, Devon

Printed and bound in Great Britain by
Clays Ltd, St Ives PLC

*British Library Cataloguing in
Publication Data*
A catalogue record for this book is
available from the British Library

*Library of Congress Cataloging in
Publication Data*
Erwin, Phil.
   Friendship in childhood and
   adolescence / Phil Erwin.
      p.   cm. – (Psychology focus)
   Includes bibliographical references
   and index
   1. Friendship in children.   2. Child
   psychology.   3. Friendship in
   adolescence.   4. Adolescent
   psychology.   I. Title.   II. Series.
   HQ784.F7E78   1998
   155.4′18—dc21   97–39543
                                 CIP

ISBN 0–415–16232–7 (hbk)

ISBN 0–415–16233–5 (pbk)

Contents

CONTENTS

Series preface

The Psychology Focus series provides short, up-to-date accounts of key areas in psychology without assuming the reader's prior knowledge in the subject. Psychology is often a favoured subject area for study, since it is relevant to a wide range of disciplines such as Sociology, Education, Nursing and Business Studies. These relatively inexpensive but focused short texts combine sufficient detail for psychology specialists with sufficient clarity for non-specialists.

The series authors are academics experienced in undergraduate teaching as well as research. Each takes a topic within their area of psychological expertise and presents a short review, highlighting important themes and including both theory and research findings. Each aspect of the topic is clearly explained with supporting glossaries to elucidate technical terms.

The series has been conceived within the context of the increasing modularisation which has been developed in higher education over the last decade and fulfils the consequent need for clear, focused, topic-based course material. Instead of following one course of study, students on a modularisation programme are often able to choose modules from a wide range of disciplines to complement the modules they are required to study for a specific degree. It can no longer be assumed that students studying for a particular module will necessarily have the same background knowledge (or lack of it!) in that subject. But they will need to familiarise themselves with a particular topic rapidly since a single module in a single topic may be only 15 weeks long, with assessments arising during that period. They may have to combine eight or more modules in a single year to obtain a degree at the end of their programme of study.

One possible problem with studying a range of separate modules is that the relevance of a particular topic or the relationship between topics may not always be apparent. In the Psychology Focus series authors have drawn where possible on practical and applied examples to support the points being made so that readers can see the wider relevance of the topic under study. Also, the study of psychology is usually broken up into separate areas, such as social psychology, developmental psychology and cognitive psychology, to take three examples. Whilst the books in the Psychology Focus series will provide excellent coverage of certain key topics within these 'traditional' areas, the authors have not been constrained in their examples and explanations and may draw on material across the whole field of psychology to help explain the topic under study more fully.

Each text in the series provides the reader with a range of important material on a specific topic. They are suitably comprehensive and give a clear account of the important issues involved. The authors analyse and interpret the material as well as present an up-to-date and detailed review of key work. Recent references are provided along with suggested further reading to allow readers to investigate the topic in more depth. It is hoped, therefore, that after following the informative review of a key topic in a Psychology Focus text, readers will not only have a clear understanding of the issues in question but will be intrigued and challenged to investigate the topic further.

Introduction and background

1

ALTHOUGH CHILDREN'S PEER RELATIONSHIPS have been the subject of research attention since at least the 1920s, it is only since the 1970s that systematic theories have been proposed to integrate the rapidly growing body of empirical knowledge. Children are involved in a variety of relationships – with parents, other adults, siblings, **peers** and so on. Two simple characteristics which distinguish children's peer relationships from their other relationships are their levels of equality and power. Relationships with peers are relationships broadly among equals. Both parties benefit from and contribute to the relationship in roughly equal measure and there is a broad balance of power. In contrast, many of a child's relationships are more hierarchically structured and are decidedly unequal. Older children and adults, especially parents, have considerably greater knowledge, resources and power and so are much more able to determine the course of a relationship and the relative outcomes for themselves and the child. The focus of this book is on children's relationships with their peers and, more specifically, children's **friendships** – their well-established reciprocal relationships with peers. However, these relationships do exist within a broader social context which includes a range of previous and current other social and personal relationships and so it is also important to bear these potential influences in mind if we are to fully understand the nature and significance of children's friendships.

In this chapter I will provide a contextual and integrative setting for the other chapters in the book. The contextual function of this chapter is fulfilled by an examination of several broad background issues. In the first section I examine the place of children's peer relationships within the child's broader social network. The subsequent sections consider the extent of children's friendship networks and even why children almost inevitably seek to form relationships with peers. A functional analysis would argue that relationships exist because they serve some generally adaptive purpose or function. Although friendship is the goal of many social relationships it is but a late stage in a more dynamic process of **acquaintanceship**. In recognition of the dynamic developmental forces within relationships some views on the sequential development of relationships are considered. Taken together, these issues lay a trail which leads to several major themes which are followed up in the remaining chapters of the book. These are briefly outlined to show how they relate to each other and the contextual issues covered in this chapter.

Friendship and other relationships

Children's earliest relationships are normally with the primary caregiver, usually the mother, and the rest of the immediate family. Throughout early childhood parents remain the major source of nurturance and the relationship that children have with their parents is closely linked to their current and future sense of well-being and happiness (Greenberg *et al.*, 1983). The significance of peer relationships increases and changes with age. For young children, relationships with parents are undoubtedly a considerably more important source of support and nurturance than are relationships with peers. From middle childhood through to adulthood this pattern changes and children's relationships with their peers become increasingly stable, intimate and personally significant, while those with parents become increasingly concerned with routine matters such as behavioural and time management issues (Furman and Buhrmester, 1992). What time they can stay out till or styles of clothing are common sources of conflict between adolescents and parents in early- and mid-adolescence. By early- to mid-adolescence, relationships with peers have overtaken those with parents as sources of intimacy and social support.

Numbers of friends

The social contacts of young children are mainly with kin. To a large extent they are dependent on their parents for any social contacts outside of the immediate family. Parents are largely responsible for arranging contacts, venues, times and transportation to meetings. These early social contacts are relatively superficial and transient but represent an important precursor and preparation for the more sophisticated relationships of later childhood onwards. Parents providing their children with such experiences are giving them an important head start on their less fortunate counterparts.

With age, the child's **social network** includes proportionately more peers and there is more daily contact with peers. Research by Feiring and Lewis (1989) on the social networks of 3- to 9-year-old children showed that even children as young as 3 often have fairly extensive social networks, on average twenty-two social contacts. By middle childhood this may have risen to thirty-nine. Although children's daily contacts generally contain more non-relatives than relatives, and more adults than peers, this pattern is likely to be more marked in older children. About a third of a child's social network may be comprised of peers, and with age children show steadily increasing levels of daily interactions with these individuals.

Children start to use the term 'best' friend at about the age of 4. At this age most children will be involved in at least one close, reciprocated peer relationship (Hinde et al., 1985), though this may be almost the full extent of the friendship network. Throughout the school years there is greater opportunity and ability to establish and maintain friendships and they increase in number from five or six at age 6 to about nine or ten at age 9 (Feiring and Lewis, 1989). However, the meaning that young children ascribe to the term 'best friend' is different from its use by older children. Throughout middle-childhood best friends may be chosen because of the demands of specific situations or occasions (Ray et al., 1995). As examples, children may have different friends at school and in the home neighbourhood, and specific individuals may be chosen when certain games are played. At this age many friendships are relatively transient, but they are also formed easily and children gain more friends than they lose (Buhrmester and Furman, 1987). With the advent of adolescence, relationships assume a new character and intimacy – and they also become considerably more irreplaceable. The overall number of close friendships possessed by an individual declines slightly as some relationships collapse and are not replaced (Hallinan, 1980).

Why form friendships?

Friendships, and peer relationships in general, serve a number of important functions for the individual. From the general literature on children's peer relationships I have compiled the list below. At any point in time a given relationship may serve one or several of these functions and different functions may be emphasised in different situations or at different points in a relationship.

Friendship motivation

There has long been a recognition by motivational theorists of a basic need for social relationships, termed variously affiliation, affection, or intimacy needs. An exponent of **humanistic psychology**, Abraham Maslow (1954), suggested a hierarchy of five needs, rising from physiological motives, through safety, love and belonging, esteem to **self-actualisation**. The lower needs were seen as more significant for survival and as appearing earlier in evolution and development. Higher motives supposedly do not appear until earlier motives have been satisfied. It is interesting to note that relationship needs appear immediately after basic physical needs. Although Maslow's theory has proved popular, some behaviour (e.g. putting yourself in danger to help another) does not seem to fit particularly well into the pattern.

McAdams and Losoff (1984) propose a specific friendship motive as a dimension of personality. They argue that to the extent that relationships satisfy this motive they possess an intrinsic reward value for the individual. Conversely, deprivation of adequate social relationships is aversive and isolated individuals may feel lonely, marginalised and depressed. Isolated and lonely individuals may fantasise about possessing fulfilling relationships and interact with others in increasingly defensive and desperate ways (Jones *et al.*, 1982).

A training ground for relationship skills

Peer relationships give children the opportunity to learn and practise their social-interaction skills with equals. In the case of friendships this includes the skills required to co-operatively build and maintain close relationships, to manage communication, conflict, trust and intimacy. Perhaps surprisingly, friends often tend to quarrel and disagree more than individuals in more casual relationships, but this may be seen as an essential training in how to manage such conflicts in a non-destructive way that will generally permit the relationship to continue and possibly even grow (Shantz, 1993). Of course, not all relationships do continue and flourish and an equally important function of children's relationships is the training they provide in how to cope with the ending of relationships that have gone wrong.

Confidence in intimacy

To a large extent, the intimacy of childhood and adolescent peer relationships may be seen as a continuation of early **attachment** relationships (Sroufe and Fleeson, 1986). However, Sullivan (1953) also highlighted preadolescence as a crucial time for the development of the first genuinely intimate peer relationships, relationships removed from the dependence on older people. Sullivan saw the close, same-sex friendships of preadolescence as crucial for the development of a sensitivity to the needs of others, our current happiness and later social adjustment. Crucially, this era and these relationships were seen as potentially repairing the damage of earlier poor relationships.

Exchanging and testing social knowledge

Again, Sullivan (1953) was an early writer to stress the role of friendships in preadolescence as an important source of insight and information about the Self. We see ourselves reflected in how others react to us. Relationships do, however, also serve as more general sources of information about others and the world in general. This informational function of relationships is likely to increase in importance with age and as the child increasingly depends on peer relationships rather than relationships with parents.

In terms of testing social knowledge, Festinger (1954) argues that there is a basic need or motivation to evaluate our abilities and attitudes. Arguably, an accurate awareness of our standing enables us to operate more effectively in our world. Many physical skills can be tested objectively. For example, we can time ourselves at running in order to evaluate our ability. However, many attitudes, values and social skills cannot be objectively evaluated and so to test these we must make **social comparisons**. An individual can evaluate his or her social abilities or attitudes by comparing them with the social abilities and attitudes held by others. This provides a **consensual validation** rather than an objective validation. It has been argued that the efficacy and social competence resulting from this consensual validation is so important and rewarding to us that we tend to seek out and associate with others who are similar to ourselves. Conversely, we may avoid and be repulsed by very dissimilar individuals. For example, the tendency for children's friends to hold similar attitudes has, at least in part, been explained in these terms (Tan and Singh, 1995). You may well have spotted that this, of course, does tend to mean that in reality we are seeking confirmation rather than a true evaluation of our attitudes and abilities!

Stimulating social cognitive development

Social and cognitive development are intimately related. As you will see throughout this book, developing cognitive abilities are the foundation on which children's relationships are built. But it also works the other way round. Social interaction can promote cognitive development. Working together, children can often solve problems which neither child could have solved on their own (Doise and Mugny, 1984). Working through a difficult problem in a free and open manner with an equal status peer can often be more instructive than being told a solution or procedure by an older child or adult.

Companionship and social support

At the very simplest level, being involved in a relationship is generally regarded as stimulating and good fun by children. They make the child a person of major importance to a figure significant in his or her social world. These friendships may serve to provide stimulation and distraction from other less attractive tasks and duties, provide assistance with difficult tasks and situations, or simply make a mundane activity more enjoyable. A task shared is often a task whose enjoyment is multiplied.

The guaranteed support of peers also protects the child against the travails of the wider social milieu, though in this they may sow the seeds of conflicts for children and parents as the parental role becomes increasingly concerned with daily care and management of the child rather than intimacy (Furman and Buhrmester, 1992). With age, peaking in adolescence, friends may increasingly provide social support for children as they question family rules and obligations, especially as they relate to issues of the child's personal or social identity (Sebald and White, 1980). Common conflicts might be over the child's style of dress, chosen companions, smoking, or perhaps the use of a social drug such as Ecstasy. Sometimes, of course, these conflicts are merely intended to test the limits of parental rules, or even simply to irritate! Despite the points that I have just made about the conflicting demands of peer groups and parents, the rebellion of adolescence is often over-exaggerated and does differ substantially from one family to another (Brookes-Gunn and Paikoff, 1992). For most teenagers, conflicts with parents are over relatively minor issues and there is typically substantial agreement on basic attitudes and values, such as educational and occupational aspirations.

Emotional buffering

Children's relationships become increasingly intimate with age and, as well as being fulfilling in their own right, they can serve to buffer or protect children against other sources of stress in their world. For example, maintaining good peer relationships may provide an emotional buffer for a child whose parents are in a discordant relationship or divorcing (Wasserstein and La Greca, 1996). The key point here is to maintain good peer relationships. Unfortunately, many stressful situations may simultaneously disrupt friendships and hence remove them as a potential source of support. Moving house or changing school, a common by-product when a child's parents divorce, also places strains on or removes supportive friendships and so serves to magnify the level of stress in the child's life.

Stages of relating

Children's relationships show both vertical and horizontal development. By vertical development I mean that relationships change as children grow older and evolve more sophisticated cognitive abilities and **social skills**. The friendships of young children show substantial differences from those of children in middle-childhood and these in turn are substantially different from those of adolescents. The vertical development factor places a ceiling on the level of sophistication and intimacy which a child can develop within any given friendship. In using the term horizontal development I am referring to the growth and change within a single, specific relationship. Levinger and Levinger (1986) see children's peer relationships as going through five broad stages, in a convenient alphabetic sequence! Many of the factors important at the different stages are examined in the succeeding chapters of this book, though it will be useful at this point to show their place in the overall pattern of relationship development:

9

Acquaintance

The initial phase in the development of a relationship is relatively superficial. A major factor at this stage is proximity, without which we are unlikely to even be aware of the other person. Most friendships tend to be formed with people who live relatively close to each other, often in the same street or neighbourhood, or who meet at specific locations, such as school, Scouts or Guides and youth clubs. With proximity comes the opportunity to develop a basic awareness of the other person based on relatively superficial factors such as their physical appearance (age, sex, race, etc.), attractiveness, artefacts (e.g. possessions and style of dress), mannerisms and patterns of behaviour. At this stage, awareness may be unilateral and the desire for further interaction and a relationship unrequited. The consequence of this stage may be that expectations are formed and interaction with the other person is desired and sought or avoided. This is very much a case of judging a book by its cover and **impression management** – controlling the image of ourselves we convey to others – can consequently be an important social skill. If initial impressions mean that another person is avoided, then there may be little opportunity for these impressions to be tested and potentially refuted. If a situation forces contact, for example in school classroom activities, this initial hurdle for the acceptance by their peers of some socially neglected children may sometimes be overcome, though it may also, of course, simply confirm an initial impression! It is no coincidence that proximity is also related to **aggression** and rejection. A disconcerting example of this is that most murderers are known to their victims! There may be some basic, relatively superficial social interaction at the acquaintance stage but the further development of a relationship takes us to the build-up phase.

Build-up

This phase represents the tentative taking of a relationship beyond superficial contact and into increasingly interconnected patterns of relating. Patterns of build-up may vary considerably. Some relationships show a gradual growth and development of patterns of interaction, others may show a sudden transition, possibly the result of some major event. Many adolescent romantic relationships are the result of some accidental circumstance which throws together two people who already know each other but did not think of each other in romantic terms. For example, a relationship may start when an individual is 'on the rebound' from another recently collapsed relationship. In this stage there is the establishment of patterns of communication, trust and reward. This is achieved through processes such as the **self-disclosure** of attitudes, opinions and interests (Rotenberg, 1995). Similarity of attitudes and many personal characteristics such as gender may be expected and sought (Kupersmidt *et al.*, 1995).

Continuation and consolidation

Once a close relationship has been established a number of other factors become important if it is to be maintained and intimacy is to be developed further. Self-disclosure continues and becomes increasingly intimate, and there are also increasing expectations that levels of self-disclosure will be reciprocated by the partner (Rotenberg and Chase, 1992). A number of other increasingly sophisticated relationship-management skills are also evident in the relationships of older children. In particular, children must learn how to manage conflict and sharing (LaFreniere, 1996). Conflict is an almost inevitable by-product of the negation of a closer relationship (Laursen, 1995). Handled successfully, it is constructive and may actually improve and push forward a relationship; handled badly it may be destructive and damaging (Burleson and Samter, 1994). With age, improving cognitive abilities and social skills allow relationships to become more stable, and loyalty, trust and feeling comfortable with intimacy also become important factors. At this stage individuals may feel more comfortable and relaxed with their partners but they are also taking on a variety of limiting obligations and commitments associated with the relationship.

Deterioration

Most relationships do not decline in a way that simply reverses their pattern of growth. At the very simplest level, it takes two to make a relationship but only one to destroy it. A number of factors may cause the deterioration in relationships. Not all relationships that deteriorate go through a phase of trauma and crisis, though this is more likely with the more involved relationships of older children and adolescents. Some children's relationships simply grow apart – for example, children's interests and attitudes may change. This may both remove the basis for the relationship and, as the children are involved with different interests and activities, result in them interacting less. External factors such as moving house may also interfere with activities that maintain the relationship. With young children they may quite simply lack the relationship-management skills to maintain a relationship over an extended period of time, or not understand and value (and hence not seek) the rewards of long-term relationships. Of course, many relationship problems are a normal and natural part of relating. Some relationships have to be lost in order that others may be gained or have room to grow in intimacy. And not all relationships that hit problems collapse. Part of the lesson taught by children's relationships is how to deal with relationship difficulties. Many children do resolve their friendship difficulties quite naturally and their relationships go on to become more stable, rewarding and enjoyable. Nonetheless, there are certainly some individuals for whom there are definite problems with relating that may impact on all their friendships, such as unrealistic expectations or inadequate social skills. For these children, psychological interventions may be necessary to avert some of the negative consequences deriving from poor peer relationships and to enable them to experience some of the positive benefits that derive from good peer relationships.

Ending

In contrast to a deterioration in the quality of a relationship, this stage marks the actual parting of the ways, the dissolution of the relationship. It is difficult for relationships simply to regress and so, if the expectations and obligations of a relationship are violated to such an extent that the relationship is no longer tenable, it is likely that interaction in general will be avoided or made formal and ritualised by the participants. Previously enjoyable encounters and joint activities may be given quite different interpretations and produce very different outcomes for the participants.

These stages within a relationship occur within the constraints of general child development and, although they broadly characterise children's relationships, are not an absolute sequence. For example, the consolidation phase is more significant in the relationships of older children and adolescents. Similarly, not all relationships are doomed to collapse, and some relationships may end without a deterioration phase, such as when a family moves home. Nonetheless, the idea of development within relationships is an important one which helps to remind us that friendships are dynamic and in a continuous process of flux and change (Hansen *et al.*, 1996). It is too easy to fall into the mistake of thinking of them in static, mechanistic terms – a fallacy that characterised much of the early literature in the area.

Integrative overview of the book

In this chapter I have provided a broad overview of children's friendships in order to introduce and provide a context for some of the more specific topics that are examined in greater detail in the subsequent chapters of this book. Chapter 2 looks at the earliest foundation upon which subsequent peer relationships are built – attachment. As Sroufe and Fleeson (1986: 52) state, 'The young child seeks and explores new relationships within the framework of expectations for self and others that emerges from the primary relationship.' This develops two points made in the first section of this chapter. First, that the various elements of a child's social network are interconnected and interdependent. Second, despite our increasing social independence from our parents over childhood and adolescence, we never fully lose the legacy of our earliest social relationship. In some way this will be reflected in all our subsequent relationships.

The next two chapters examine the cognitive and behavioural bases of children's friendships. Chapter 3 focuses on the social cognitive bases of children's peer relationships. Initially, it is concerned with how babies and young children become aware of themselves as individuals, differentiate themselves from others, and develop an awareness of others as individuals with thoughts and feelings. These differentiations are an obvious prerequisite for any social relationship to be possible. Later social cognitive processes become the filters through which children's social experiences are passed. Experiences are interpreted, they are subject to a variety of expectations and attributional biases, and these interpretations guide children's social behaviours. The processes that influence these interpretations are crucial to successful and fulfilling social interaction; they also underlie what are considered the appropriate behavioural responses to social events. Cognitive abilities and interactional skills are essentially two sides of the same coin. They are mutually influencing and a basic competence in both domains is necessary for successful social relationships. Chapter 4 is concerned with the interactional bases of children's friendships and peer relationships. The ability to establish and effectively manage social interaction is an important social skill. A generally positive orientation with flexible and sensitive communication skills underlies much social success, though even conflict can promote relationship development if handled constructively. Boys and girls may differ in what they seek from their relationships and hence how they are managed. The common sex segregation in children's relationships is also explored in this chapter.

In Chapter 5 I turn to a specific focus on adolescence. A major concern of this chapter is how the sex segregation of middle-childhood is resolved. The emergence and development of cross-sex relationships is examined. Throughout childhood and approaching adolescence, children adopt a variety of strategies for managing occasional cross-sex encounters and these come to provide a foundation on which cross-sex relationships of adolescence are built. Having covered the major background material relevant to a general understanding of children's and adolescents' peer relationships, Chapter 6 tries to add just a little bit of complication into the picture by examining how the context in which relationships are lived out may affect them. This is very much in line with current approaches in social and developmental psychology which stress the understanding of natural behaviour, not just behaviour in highly controlled laboratory conditions. Relationships are considerably more influenced by social and environmental conditions than much early research acknowledged. Continuing the 'real world' theme, Chapter 7 is concerned with relationship problems in otherwise normal and well-adjusted children. Although this is still a very fragmented area, we are beginning to understand the nature of **loneliness, shyness,** social isolation and general relationship problems throughout childhood. Importantly, we are also beginning to recognise that relationship problems in childhood do have important implications for later happiness and social adjustment.

Chapter 8, the final chapter, closes the book on an optimistic note, for its main message is that there is now a wealth of approaches by which children may be helped to improve their relationships. Just as relationship problems are many and varied, so also are the variety of therapeutic approaches that have been shown to be effective in their remediation. These methods of promoting positive peer relationships are also starting to come out of the research centres and find their ways into schools. School counsellors and Personal and Social Education programmes are increasingly giving attention to human relationships. Importantly, prevention is increasingly being recognised as a better and more successful strategy for resolving relationship difficulties than trying later in life to repair dysfunctional patterns of relating. There may be a long way to go, but research on methods of improving children's peer relationships is well under way and growing rapidly.

Summary

This chapter provided an overview of the nature and significance of children's peer relationships. Initially, children's peer relationships, and especially friendships, were distinguished from the wide variety of relationships that children also have with other social figures. Although peer relationships become increasingly important throughout childhood, they are nonetheless but one part of a broader social network and exist within the context, demands and support of these other relationships. This naturally raised the question of how extensive are children's circles of friends. Studies are reasonably concordant in the numbers of friends that they report children as having. Typically, there are about five or six in young schoolchildren and rising to nine or ten by age 9. More interesting is the finding that friendship circles slightly decrease from preadolescence onwards. The initial increase arguably reflects the increasing stability of children's relationships, the subsequent decline may represent the irreplaceablility of the intimate, demanding relationships of adolescence. So, with friendships representing a major part of children's lives, it would seem likely that they are serving some important function. In fact, children's peer relationships serve many functions. I discussed seven major functions: to satisfy an intrinsic friendship motivation; as a training ground for social skills; to give the child confidence in intimacy; to allow children to exchange and test their social knowledge; to stimulate social cognitive development; to provide companionship and social support; to act as an emotional buffer.

Moving on from general issues, I distinguished two aspects of relationship development. First, is vertical development: that the level of sophistication of children's friendships changes with age. Second, is horizontal patterns of development: this is the pattern of development within a specific relationship. A child's level of vertical development will impose a ceiling on the level of horizontal development that is possible in a child's current friendships. Levinger and Levinger's (1986) five-stage model of relationship development was outlined. The stages of acquaintance, build-up, continuation, deterioration and ending were used to organise a discussion of the patterns of growth in children's friendships. A number of important aspects of the development of children's relationships were raised in the chapter and I concluded by outlining how some of these are followed up in more detail in the subsequent chapters of the book.

Further reading

Frønes, I. (1995). *Among peers: on the meaning of peers in the process of socialization.* Boston, MA: Scandinavian University Press. This is an interesting and very readable book that is refreshingly different from the style of most other texts in this area. Its thoughtful analysis tries to broaden the psychological perspective by also drawing on sociology and history.

Hartup, W. W. and Stevens, N. (1997). Friendship and adaptation in the life course. *Psychological Bulletin*, 121, 355–70. This is the latest in a series of essays by a leading authority on children's peer relationships. It considers the different levels of analysis which may be applied to an understanding of children's friendships and the implications of different dimensions of friendship for later adaptation.

Chapter 2

Attachment and later relationships

ALTHOUGH ATTACHMENT IS A LONG-ESTABLISHED area of psychological research, it has been characterised by major controversies throughout most of its history. Indeed, authors from different theoretical orientations find it difficult even to agree on a definition of attachment! Given this state of affairs, it is appropriate that the definition of attachment is an early issue discussed in this chapter. Having considered this fundamental question, the chapter then provides a basic introduction to attachment theory and research. Fundamental questions are addressed, such as how do children become attached to their parents? How can we measure attachment? And, how do patterns of attachment vary from one child to another? These are important questions but even more significant is the potential impact of attachment on children's subsequent relationships. The final section of the chapter focuses on the impact of early attachment on later peer relationships throughout childhood and adolescence.

Background

Biologically, attachment is a mechanism designed to protect and promote the adaptive development of the child, and hence preserve the species. The attachment figure provides a safe base from which the child can explore and learn about a complex and potentially dangerous world, and a source of comfort and reassurance in times of stress and hurt. The initial attachment of a child to its mother, or other primary caregiver, is both the foundation upon which subsequent relationships are built and, more pervasively, provides a **working model** or set of expectations that intimately determine how subsequent relationships are constructed and managed. When securely attached children learn to trust and rely on their relationships with their mothers, they are developing positive and persistent expectations that these characteristics can and probably will be achieved in other relationships. To these children, relationships are satisfying and fulfilling. In contrast, children with poor attachment histories may become anxious and over-dependent and are also likely to carry the baggage of their expectations forward to their subsequent relationships. As Sroufe (1979) states, 'We cannot assume that early experiences will somehow be cancelled by later experience. Lasting consequences of early inadequate experience may be subtle and complex . . . But there will be consequences.' For these children there may be lifelong difficulties in fully committing themselves and trusting in their relationships. Equally significantly, research suggests that children learn both sides of the attachment relationship and thus when they themselves become parents they may recreate the pattern of their own inadequate and damaging experiences (e.g. DeKlyen, 1996). By these means, patterns of deprived and neglectful parenting may be transmitted through successive generations of a family.

Class, culture and patterns of adaptation

The connection between early attachment and later relationship functioning has, in the main, been established by research on the mother–child relationship of middle-class Americans and Europeans. It is important that we are aware of the cultural and evaluative biases implicit in much of the child-rearing literature so that we can at least avoid unwarranted and dangerous generalisations of findings to other social groups, classes and cultures. A specific type of mother–child relationship that produces well-adapted adults in one social situation may be far from adaptive in another. This is nicely illustrated by Ogbu's (1981) study, which showed that social survival for American ghetto children required very different patterns of behaviour from that expected of their middle-class counterparts. For the ghetto children, gang membership and being generally 'streetwise' was more important than scholastic achievement. Ghetto parents tended to be extremely warm and affectionate to their infants but also used an

authoritarian style of parenting, which was severe, inconsistent, power-assertive and used physical punishment. This produced a pattern of behaviours which, while frowned on by the middle classes, was highly adaptive in the ghetto: assertiveness, self-reliance and a mistrust of authority figures. In contrast, middle-class parents are more likely to use an **authoritative style of parenting** based on the explanation and negotiation of rules of behaviour. Self-control and non-physical styles of discipline are likely to be stressed. The message is simple: different styles of parenting may be adaptive in different circumstances.

I hope that this brief overview has shown how important early attachment is in all our early lives and for our later adjustment. For it to be a useful concept we also need to be able to define and measure attachment. It is to the definition of attachment that I turn next.

Defining attachment

The major value of attachment is as an integrative concept; it allows a simple explanation for the relationship between various attachment behaviours and the continuity of these behaviours over time and different situations. But opinions are sharply divided as to whether we should make the inferential leap from overt behaviours to an assumption of some underlying entity. The term attachment has been used in two fundamentally different ways.

Originally, the term attachment was used to refer to the intense and enduring emotional or affective bond of an individual to one or a few significant others. An important point to note here is that from this perspective the attachment bond is a characteristic of the individual child. The child is attached to the mother. Attachment is not seen as a characteristic of the dyad, of the pair of relators (Ainsworth, 1989). Attachment is seen as the underlying force that drives the diverse attachment behaviours that we see and that serve to maintain proximity with the attachment figure.

Other authors have been less willing to make the inferential leap from observed social behaviours to underlying emotional bonds. From their perspective, the term attachment is simply a metaphor denoting a particular class of responses, such as separation anxiety and proximity-seeking, that characterise some relationships (Gewirtz and Pelaez-Nogueras, 1991). As a metaphor, attachment is simply a convenient summary term indicating a characteristic type of interaction rather than an underlying cause for these patterns of behaviour; it is a characteristic of the interaction rather than the individual.

Becoming attached

Both the mother and the infant play crucial roles in establishing and maintaining a strong and secure attachment relationship. The child affects attachment mainly via the impact its appearance, temperament and responsiveness have on the responsiveness of the caregiver.

Caregivers affect attachment mainly through their acceptance, sensitivity and responsiveness to the child (Kochanska, 1997). Current family circumstances may play an important role here. Stressful changes such as unemployment or illness can affect patterns of maternal care and hence attachment status (Pianta et al., 1989). On the positive side, supportive relationships with family and friends may buffer against these effects. An interesting factor that appears to be an important influence on the mother's responsiveness to her infant is her own childhood family experiences. Mothers experiencing major difficulties with their toddlers are themselves likely to come from disrupted families (e.g. where parents were divorced) or have had poor relations with their parents (Main et al., 1985). Taken to extremes, parents from a background of neglect or abuse also seem more inclined to misinterpret natural infant behaviours as difficult or rejecting and are at risk of mistreating their child (Youngblade and Belsky, 1989). Although many of the supposed cross-generational effects of attachment are inferred from the retrospective or anecdotal accounts of the individuals concerned, more objective evidence for a link between the cognitive representations of relationships of mothers and their children is accumulating (Burks and Parke, 1996). This is spurring on attempts to break the cycle of maladaptation. A number of intervention studies, with varying degrees of success, have tried to promote sensitive patterns of parenting in order to produce secure attachment in children and so break these intergenerational cycles of insecure attachments (Juffer *et al.*, 1997).

A chronology of attachment

In the first few months of life the child does not show attachment as such but does show patterns of preference and behaviour that promote the proximity of other people, especially the mother, and facilitate later attachments. For example, the newborn child prefers the sound of the human voice and can even discriminate and prefers the mother's voice. On the part of the caregiver, behaviours such as sucking, smiling, clinging, visual attention and crying on separation are interpreted as signs of content, and as confirmation of good parenting: they are likely to promote positive feelings and the desire for further contact. From about 6 weeks of age the child shows a distinct preference for social rather than non-social stimuli and, having learnt the consequences of its natural behaviours, uses some of them instrumentally. Crying, for example, may be used as a social signal in order to attract attention. Despite the child's obviously social orientation by this age, there is still no consistent preference for one specific caregiver rather than another.

Over the next several months the infant gradually becomes more discriminating in its attachment behaviours. Proximity-promoting behaviours are still directed at a variety of people, though infants react more positively to the people who regularly take care of them. At about 6 or 7 months of age the child achieves a major milestone in its social development: the formation of the primary attachment. Attachment behaviours are now starting to be focused on the primary caregiver and a fear of strange adults emerges. Interestingly, stranger-anxiety towards unfamiliar children develops considerably later, at about 2 years of age, reflecting the lesser contact a child has with its peers and hence the lesser opportunity to develop a **schema** for children's faces. Once the child is able to crawl it does not have to totally rely on the caregiver to maintain proximity. With its greater mobility the child is also able to explore wider afield, while using the caregiver as a secure base in case it feels threatened and has the need to retreat because of, say, the arrival of a strange adult.

As the child approaches the end of its first year its explorations are becoming increasingly extensive and its social world is widening. There begins a **generalisation** of attachment to include other significant figures, such as the father and siblings, and stranger-anxiety starts to decline. On encountering new people, objects and situations, the reactions of attachment figures may be used for **social referencing,** as a guide for the child's own reactions (Rosen *et al.,* 1992). Some authors have even gone so far as to argue that social referencing is an early indicator of the child's emerging theory of mind, showing that the child has a basic awareness of others as distinct psychological entities (Bretherton, 1984). This is a prerequisite for more sophisticated, genuinely interpersonal relationships. Children's Theories of Mind are discussed further in Chapter 3.

As the child develops beyond its first year, peers gradually become increasingly important in the child's life. Nonetheless, through most of childhood and into preadolescence parental attachments do remain of central, if less obvious significance to the child. Parents are still seen as the main source of nurturance and this is most evident in exceptional circumstances, for example homesickness. Until quite late in childhood, and even into early adolescence, quality of attachment to parents seems to be more closely related to a sense of well-being and happiness than is quality of relationships with peers (Greenberg *et al.,* 1983). The monopolistic significance of parental attachments does decline throughout adolescence, though it has been argued that their impact is never fully escaped (Ainsworth, 1989).

This section has provided a basic introduction to the origins of attachment, the child's first genuine social relationship. However, for researchers to conduct meaningful research in the area it has been necessary to devise methods by which attachment can be accurately measured. It is to this issue that I turn next.

Measuring attachment

For it to be a useful notion we need to be able to operationally define attachment, i.e. to specify procedures for measuring attachment. According to John Bowlby (1969), attachment is indicated by a number of behaviours which serve to promote frequent interaction and maintain proximity. Such behaviours include crying, smiling, clinging to the attachment figure and following the attachment figure. Although we could assess a child's attachment status through a long-term observation of its interactions with its caregivers, this would be a difficult and expensive approach to the problem. An easier, quicker and more direct strategy is to devise a test to assess this behaviour. One of the most widely used and accepted tests of attachment for infants of 12–18 months of age is the **Strange Situations Test** (Ainsworth *et al.*, 1978), which I will now examine.

The Strange Situations Test

In the Strange Situations Test an infant is observed for a period of up to 21 minutes in a room scattered with toys. In this room the child's reactions are observed when it is left on its own, with its mother, with the mother and a stranger, and on its own with a stranger. Most crucial are the child's reactions to being separated from and then reunited with the mother. The child's attachment style is inferred from the patterns of behaviour observed during the various separations and reunions. The Strange Situations Test has proved a popular research tool and there is now a substantial body of evidence showing clear patterns of attachment behaviours in specific situations, good levels of reliability when children who were securely attached at 1 year of age were retested at 18 months and 6 years of age (Main *et al.*, 1985), and good links between attachment classifications and previously observed mother–child interaction in the home in the first few months of the child's life.

Despite its widespread use, a number of important criticisms have been raised against the Strange Situations Test and its classifications of attachment. Many of the behaviours that are shown in these situations have had their selectivity questioned, especially their power to discriminate between an attachment figure and some other familiar, non-feared person. Similarly problematic are questions that have been raised over the stability and reliability of attachment classifications (Belsky *et al.*, 1996). Some children show different patterns of attachment when judged on the basis of one behavioural index rather than another (e.g. crying on separation, following, gaze), may change their attachment classification with a change in family circumstances, show different patterns of behaviour from one day to the next, and behave differently in some familiar situations, such as the home, rather than in unfamiliar situations such as developmental laboratories and observation rooms!

At least two main factors may be contributing to the apparent difficulties in measuring attachment. First, the role of temperament seems to have been under-estimated (Seifer *et al.*, 1996). Some children are more temperamentally irritable, anxious or independent than others and their attachment classification may reflect these traits. Having said this, it has been argued that the way a caregiver responds to an infant, rather than its temperament as such, may still be the major influence on attachment: a baby's temperament is, of course, likely to promote specific patterns of childcare from its parents (Buss and Plomin, 1984). For example, irritable children may exhaust their parents and reduce their tolerance and responsiveness, or else may encourage over-control or indulgence. To draw these arguments to a conclusion, infant temperament and patterns of caregiving are inextricably intertwined and mutually influencing. Nonetheless, infant behaviours in the first few weeks of life, such as levels of crying, are not in themselves particularly predictive of later attachment: maternal responsiveness is.

A second potential problem with the Strange Situations Test as a measure of attachment is that it does not sufficiently acknowledge patterns of socialisation as determinants of children's responses. Some parents may stress independence and play down overly demonstrative displays of emotion. Children raised with these **display rules** may miscue an observer as to the nature of their relationship with their mother. This idea is supported by evidence from cross-cultural studies which show substantial differences in the proportions of children apparently showing various types of attachment. Cultural norms and values can substantially bias the results of the Strange Situations Test and have even led to a questioning of its cross-cultural validity (Nakagawa *et al.*, 1992).

Quality of attachment

Three main types or qualities of attachment are typically distinguished: secure attachment, insecure-avoidant attachment, and insecure-resistant attachment. Each of these patterns of attachment is the product of a specific parenting style and will be outlined in turn.

Secure attachment

Secure attachment is typically the result of warm, responsive patterns of childcare. The mothers of securely attached children appear to enjoy touching and close contact with their child, are sensitive to the child's needs and encourage the infant to explore and communicate. The securely attached child appears open and receptive to the mother's social overtures and *expects* the mother to be responsive to its needs and overtures. The securely attached child shows a clear preference for the mother in comparison to strangers and although it enjoys proximity it is not clinging. The securely attached child uses the mother as a safe base for active exploration, maintaining contact through occasional glances towards her. While the mother is present the child is socially outgoing to strangers but is visibly upset if separated from the mother; on her return the mother is greeted warmly and with evident pleasure and the child is comforted if distressed. Of 1 year olds, 50–70 per cent are typically classified as securely attached and have a sound basis for their subsequent relationships.

Insecure-avoidant attachment

This style of attachment is often characterised by a lack of responsiveness to the child's demands and a tendency to eschew physical contact; mother–child interactions are often brief and unrewarding. These mothers are often rigid, relatively intolerant and self-centred people who are likely to reject their babies if they are temperamentally difficult or interfere with their own lives and plans. These children learn to return the mother's behaviour in kind, they do not actively seek contact with her and do not show marked signs of distress when separated from her. The superficiality of the child's relationship with the mother does not encourage the child to regard her as a source of security and so the child shows little interest or confidence in using her as a base from which to explore its world. The child does not show any marked fear of strangers, treating them to a large extent in the same way it treats the mother – often ignoring or avoiding them. Of 1 year olds, 20–25 per cent are typically classified as showing insecure-avoidant attachment. An interesting paradox about this attachment classification is that it can also result from a mother being too attentive (Isabella and Belsky, 1991). Avoidance can be a way of regulating a mother's excessive and insensitive pressures for interaction.

Insecure-resistant attachment

The mothers of these children do attempt to provide close physical contact but often appear to have problems in interpreting their infant's needs. Consequently, they may be inconsistent and unresponsive to their child's needs. The child also shows inconsistent and ambivalent patterns of behaviour, at times appearing dependent and clinging and at other times avoiding or even fighting against contact. The lack of confidence in the mother as a safe base also makes the child appear anxious, reluctant to explore and, even in the presence of the mother, very suspicious of strangers. Although the resistant child has a far from perfect relationship with its mother, it is very distressed if the mother departs. But, on being reunited, the ambivalent nature of the relationship with the mother again presents itself: the child is angry about the enforced separation and both seeks comfort from the mother yet resists her attempts to provide this comfort, possibly pushing her away or even trying to hit her. The result of these conflicting motives and behaviours is that the child is likely to remain near the mother but resist any attempt at physical contact. This type of attachment characterises about 10 per cent of 1 year olds and is more common in infants who were temperamentally difficult babies.

Attachment and children's peer relationships

Research in this area has most commonly focused on the impact of early attachments on young children's abilities and social orientation in other current and future relationships, though there is also a growing body of research that has attempted to look at the effects of current parental attachments on the personal and social adjustment and friendships of older children and adolescents (e.g. Krollmann and Krappmann, 1996).

The preschool years

The impact of early attachment on subsequent relationships is most clearly shown in those peer relationships that are formed soonest after the primary attachment. These are less coloured by other influences. The relationship between an infant's security of attachment to its primary caregiver and the quality of its subsequent close peer relationships throughout the preschool years and into the nursery school is well documented (Youngblade and Belsky, 1992). In comparison to infants classified as insecurely attached, infants classified as securely attached appear to be more co-operative, friendly and outgoing with other children and adults. They are more skilful and effective with their peers, not easily frustrated and are better able to cope with defusing interpersonal conflicts. The overall effect of this style of behaviour is that children from a background of secure attachment tend to be more sought after as friends and partners in play (LaFreniere and Sroufe, 1985). In contrast, insecure-avoidant toddlers tend to be more distant and negative in their orientation to peers. Even if they do try to participate in ongoing play, they are more likely to elicit aggression and rejection from their partners. Preschooler victimisation and being bullied is often associated with a history of avoidant attachment (Troy and Sroufe, 1987). The inadequacies of the insecure-resistant child are also distinctive. They may show more attempts at social participation than insecure-avoidant or securely attached children, but their lack of skill makes many of their overtures appear impulsive, over-assertive and ineffective. Of the three attachment classifications, these children are likely to be lowest in peer status (LaFreniere and Sroufe, 1985). In the nursery school, insecure-resistant children may show chronic low-level helplessness and dependency and their lack of success with peers may lead them to be constantly near or orientated to the teacher (Sroufe, 1983). Overall, even if they do make considerable efforts in their social overtures to their peers, insecurely attached children are more likely to receive disruptive, rejecting responses.

So far I have discussed the impact of a child's attachment history on its social skills and social orientation, mainly in initial encounters and often with a strange partner. But, of course, an interaction involves at least two individuals and it may lead to a more extensive relationship. Fortunately, research has investigated the effect of mutual quality of attachment on later longer-term relationships. In a study of pairs of 4-year-old friends, Kerns (1994) found that interactions were more positive when both children were classified as securely attached than when one member

31

was insecurely attached. When the children's relationships were reassessed a year later, this was again confirmed. The main implication here is that skilful, securely attached children will find it most rewarding to interact with each other; the insecurely attached children, who would benefit and learn most from interacting with a more skilful peer, are unlikely to have this opportunity. The stage is already being set for the establishment of social cliques that will inevitably perpetuate and increase the skills differences and hence quality of social experiences that exist between securely and insecurely attached children.

School and beyond

The evidence for the impact of early attachments on the subsequent peer relationships of older children and adolescents shows a considerable consistency with the patterns observed in preschoolers. Note, however, that many studies of attachment in older populations ask participants either to self-assess their current attachment status or to retrospectively report on their earlier attachment experiences (e.g. Kerns *et al.*, 1996). Studies based on either of these approaches can be somewhat difficult to interpret as the direction of causality is often unclear. Do people report a strong, secure parental attachment because they are currently experiencing positive peer relationships, or are their positive peer relationships a reflection of their positive attachments? Or perhaps both patterns of relating are a reflection of some other factor in the person's life!

A long-term study that has followed the same children for over a decade has found that the differences in social competence that have been discussed in the preceding sections are relatively stable characteristics (Sroufe and Jacobvitz, 1989). Ten year olds with a background of secure attachment scored significantly higher on several measures of social competence and adjustment and significantly lower on dependence, they were less often isolated and less likely to be the passive recipients of aggression. Supporting this, in a study of thirty-two preadolescents at a four-week summer camp, Shulman *et al.* (1994) found higher levels of peer competence in children who had been securely attached to their caregivers as infants, and corresponding differences in the quality of the friendships they established while at camp. These studies show a considerable degree of consistency with the earlier findings from the studies of children up to the age of 5.

As the child enters adolescence, peers become an increasingly important reference group, though the relationships with parents continue to be the base from which the many new and conflicting demands of a rapidly expanding social world can be explored. Indeed, until relatively late in adolescence, quality of relationships with parents may continue to be more important for the individual's well-being, self-esteem and happiness than those with peers. A number of studies have confirmed the relationship between current security of attachment and adolescent self-esteem (e.g. Paterson *et al.*, 1995). These effects may also impact on peer relationships. Kerns and Stevens (1996) found that late adolescents' maternal attachments were related to a measure of loneliness and the quantity and quality of daily interactions but, interestingly, not the quality of friendships. No doubt this is a topic that will receive substantial further research attention and the full meaning of these results will be clarified.

Summary

This chapter examined the nature of attachment and its implications for the subsequent peer relationships of children and adolescents. I initially looked at how different researchers viewed attachment as either an emotional bond or as a metaphor for certain characteristic patterns of relating. I then went on to examine how attachments are formed, including the influence of personal, social and cross-generational factors. Moving on to look at the measurement of attachment, I focused on the Strange Situations Test, which is based on the idea that children's responses during separations from and reunions with their caregivers can indicate the quality of their attachments. The Strange Situations Test has been severely criticised. In particular, it has been argued that the role of a child's temperament has been under-estimated as a factor in attachment classifications. Despite the many criticisms, and undoubted other influences on attachment classifications, the Strange Situations Test has become a major means of determining the quality of a young child's attachment.

In the remaining sections of this chapter I focused on the impact and continuity of attachment with later relationships. Although still a matter of contention by some authors, there is now substantial evidence that quality of attachment to caregivers is reflected in the subsequent social orientation and quality of peer relationships of preschool and school-age children. Attachment has also been found to be an important predictor of adolescent self-esteem and social involvement, though studies with this age group have tended to examine attachment in terms of either retrospective assessments or current patterns of relationships with parents.

Further reading

Fox, N. (1995). Of the way we were: adult memories about attachment experiences and their role in determining infant–parent relationships: a commentary on van Ijzendoorn (1995). *Psychological Bulletin*, 117, 404–10.

van Ijzendoorn, M. H. (1995). Of the way we were: on temperament, attachment, and the transmission gap: a rejoinder to Fox (1995). *Psychological Bulletin*, 117, 411–15.

van Ijzendoorn, M. H. (1995). Adult attachment representations, parental responsiveness, and infant attachment: a meta-analysis on the predictive validity of the adult attachment interview. *Psychological Bulletin*, 117, 387–403. Most psychologists would accept that our early attachment experiences may impact on the way we respond to our own young children. Rather than trying to retrospectively assess the impact of actual attachment experiences on caregivers, much recent attachment research has focused on the individual's current interpretation and structuring of these experiences. This recent empirical review of research demonstrates the association between parental representations of attachment, parental responsiveness and the quality of current parent–infant attachments. To give a balanced evaluation of the arguments and conclusions presented, it is also useful to read the brief commentary on this article, and rejoinder, in the same issue of the journal.

Parke, R. D. and Ladd, G. W. (eds) (1992). *Family–peer relationships: modes of linkage*. Hillsdale, NJ: Erlbaum. A fairly comprehensive review of the linkages between two important domains of developmental psychology. It examines both direct and indirect influences as well as several less commonly discussed topics such as peer relations in maltreated children and the effects of depressed caregivers.

Chapter 3

Social cognitive bases of children's peer relationships

SOCIAL COGNITION IS CONCERNED WITH 'how children conceptualise other people and how they come to understand the thoughts, emotions, intentions, and viewpoints of others' (Shantz, 1975: 258). **Social cognitive** processes enable children to predict the behaviour of others, control their own behaviour, and consequently attempt to regulate their social interactions (Slomkowski and Dunn, 1996). In other words, children's social behaviour is mediated by their social cognitive processes and, although these processes are far from complete in the explanation they provide for social behaviour, the basis for an individual's actions cannot be fully understood without taking them into account. A simple example will make this point clearer: if a child is tripped by another child in a school playground, the response that will follow is likely to depend on whether the act is interpreted as accidental or deliberately aggressive.

In this review I will focus on six broad, interrelated aspects of social cognitive development that are important in children's relationships: the development of a sense of personal identity or Self, **empathy, role-taking,** theories of mind, friendship concepts and attributions of causality. The child's development of a personal identity or sense of Self is an important basis from which one can also develop a concept of others as independent beings. Empathy, role-taking and a theory of mind explain how children come to understand another person's psychological state and social perspective. These abilities make interpersonal relationships possible and are important if one is to relate to others effectively. The child's level of understanding of the concept of friendship, and the rules and obligations entailed by such a relationship, is an important topic because friendship expectations will affect how the behaviour of other children is interpreted. These interpretations may facilitate or inhibit the establishment of a new relationship or determine the future course of a current relationship. Finally, the causal attributions children make to explain the behaviour of others, understanding whether another's behaviour was freely chosen or due simply to luck or circumstances, is crucial in evaluating the behaviour relative to the expectations and obligations of a relationship. Different interpretations may produce very different behavioural responses and social outcomes. In combination, these topics emphasise that to form successful relationships the child must have a sense of Self as distinct from others, appreciate that others are unique individuals with a distinct social perspective, possess expectations and criteria which distinguish friendship behaviour from other social behaviour, and be able to infer whether apparently friendly behaviour was intended. I will now examine each of these topics in more detail.

A sense of Self

The individual's awareness of Self and social development are interdependent. A sense of Self is only possible if the child also recognises that there is a world of non-Self. An awareness of Self as a distinct, independent entity makes relationships possible, but the Self is also defined by, and dynamically reflected in, the individual's developing social relationships. We gain part of our identity from the way people react to us and our behaviour. This is what Cooley (1912) memorably termed 'the looking-glass self'.

There have been many debates about the age at which infants achieve a sense of Self. Most authors argue that it takes several months for the newborn to acquire clear sense of Self, though even 1-day-old children can synchronise their head movements with those of an adult, which suggests a basic awareness of themselves as entities separate and distinct from their environment. Throughout the next few months this basic awareness undergoes considerable development and refinement as children become increasingly aware of themselves as active agents in their world. They may fake cries simply to attract attention or enjoy creating movement in mobiles.

By 1 year of age children are already able to discriminate men from women and babies from adults – and prefer to play with another infant (Lewis and Brooks-Gunn, 1979). By 2 years of age children are using language in ways which give a direct insight to the status of their self-concept. By this age, some toddlers are already using 'I', 'me' and 'you' to refer to themselves and others (Lewis and Brooks-Gunn, 1979). The child recognises its unique identity and that others have separate identities. During the preschool years these discriminative abilities become increasingly refined and are reflected in the increasing selectivity and sophistication of children's relationships.

Throughout childhood and into adolescence children's thinking and self-concepts become increasingly complex. Young children will generally describe themselves in terms of their name, age, sex, address and perhaps one or two major features or significant interests or activities. By adolescence these self-definitions have become considerably more differentiated and abstract. Adolescents will typically define themselves in terms of traits, beliefs, motivations and interpersonal affiliations. Even if young children do use trait terms, they use them in qualitatively different ways to adolescents: they are seen as concrete and unchanging. To a young child, the description 'nice' is seen as a relatively permanent and invariant characteristic of a person's behaviour; to the adolescent, it may be regarded as a personality trait which is limited by situation and circumstance.

Empathy

Empathy plays a significant role in interpersonal communication and relationships. Empathy has been defined as 'an affective response more appropriate to someone else's situation than to one's own' (Hoffman, 1987: 48). There is some evidence that a basic empathic ability is innate, as shown in the contagion of crying evident even in children less than 36 hours old. Additional evidence comes from the study of twins. Identical twins show moderately similar levels of empathic concern, but there is little evidence of this in fraternal twins (Matthews *et al.*, 1981).

Young children vicariously experiencing the arousal of others will initially be unable to distinguish it from their own arousal. In attempting to understand their own reactions they are learning to distinguish themselves from others, and will be taking the first steps in learning to understand the different feelings of others. This conceptualisation emphasises the affective nature of empathic understanding, but does not imply that the affective response is or need be identical to that of the other person.

Although affect is the defining feature of empathy, empathic ability is also closely correlated with general cognitive development. Simple empathy is the foundation on which more sophisticated cognitive role-taking abilities are built, though later it is the child's cognitive abilities that set the limits for the development of more advanced forms of empathy. In the development of empathy there is a gradual move from an emphasis on the immediate, superficial and obvious concordance of emotional reactions towards an emphasis on the inferred, abstract qualities which underpin the response. Although cognitive processes set the limits for empathy, this does imply that they determine responsiveness. With equal levels of understanding there may be marked variations in empathy: for example, it is likely to be greater towards others who are perceived as similar on some dimension significant for the individual, such as age, sex, or ethnic background.

Development of empathy

Martin Hoffman (1988) has proposed a four-stage model of the development of empathy. In the first year of life there is a global empathy, the automatic matching of emotion: for example, children often cry in response to hearing another infant crying. This stage reflects the very young children's lack of discrimination between themselves and others. Children at stage 2, approximately 1 to 3 years of age, have more sophisticated cognitive abilities, especially role-taking abilities, and show a fuller understanding of the basis of their empathic feelings. Children at this stage display an egocentric empathy. The familiarity of a situation may be the crucial determinant of a young child's ability to recognise and empathise with the affective state of another (Barnett, 1984). This is a primitive form of empathy, possibly based on stereotypes or the child's memory of similar experiences and their associated emotional consequences. Children empathising with the personal distress of another may try to offer comfort in ways which they would find personally comforting. For example, an 18-month-old child may fetch his or her own mother to comfort a crying companion even though the other child's mother is also present. Stage 3 sees the gradual emergence of a true empathic under-standing. By middle-childhood the child can cope with the simultaneous display of contradictory emotions, and responses are becoming increasingly subtle. For example, a child may empathise with another's distress but also appreciate that providing help could cause embarrassment and would not be appreciated. Despite their apparent sophistication, these empathic abilities are still limited to concrete situations. In the final stage of the develop-ment of empathy, beginning in adolescence, children show an increasing ability to use personal and psychological reasons rather than situational descriptions in explaining the emotions of others and their own empathic responses. There is the potential for a deeper, more general appreciation of the long-term effects and implications of another's circumstances, such as the death of a family member, and there can also be empathic concern for entire groups or classes of people, such as the poor or handicapped. As adolescent relationships increasingly emphasise intimacy and involvement, empathic abilities at this stage have major implica-tions for peer evaluations of social competence. Higher levels of empathic understanding are associated with greater popularity and more satisfying peer relationships.

Role-taking

In order to understand and effectively relate to others it is neces-sary to appreciate that they possess a different perspective from our own. Role-taking is the term given to the ability to see the world from another person's perspective. Good role-taking abilities enable the individual to anticipate other people's needs, perceptions and actions, and to take the other's viewpoint into account when making interpersonal judgements or deciding on interpersonal behaviours. More mature patterns of role-taking are associated with lower levels of aggressiveness and more positive, pro-social behaviour towards peers, such as sharing and helping. Little surprise then that research shows significant correlations between a child's level of role-taking skills, their likelihood of sustaining reciprocal friendships and general peer popularity, especially in older children.

Even young preschoolers have a basic understanding that another's perspective differs from their own and can recognise basic emotions in others (Denham, 1986), though these abilities are refined throughout childhood and extraneous factors such as social class and familiarity with the test situation may bias the apparent age at which various levels of skill are acquired. The major theoretical explanation of role-taking, based on Piaget's cognitive developmental theory, was proposed by Selman (1980), and it is this that I will outline next.

Selman investigated the development of children's social cognitive abilities by means of a series of semi-structured interviews. Children were typically presented with a social dilemma, a story without an ending, and then led into a probing discussion around a set of key questions. Undoubtedly the limitations of his methodology, as with Piaget's original research, may underestimate the abilities of young children, though of most significance is the sequential order in which role-taking abilities are acquired rather than their specific age of onset. When age ranges are mentioned they are to be regarded merely as rough guidelines! A sample dilemma used with 4–10 year olds, and its associated key questions (from Selman), is presented below:

> Holly is an 8-year-old girl who likes to climb trees. She is the best tree climber in the neighbourhood. One day while climbing down from a tall tree, she falls off the bottom branch but does not hurt herself. Her father sees her fall. He is upset and asks her to promise not to climb trees any

more. Holly promises. Later that day, Holly and her friends meet Sean. Sean's kitten is caught up in a tree and can't get down. Something has to be done right away, or the kitten may fall. Holly is the only one who climbs trees well enough to reach the kitten and get it down, but she remembers her promise to her father.

(Selman, 1980: 36–7)

The role-taking questions associated with the above story focused on the point of view of each character in the story, the relationship between the perspectives of the different characters in the story, and conflicts within the subject's own point of view. Typical questions for this dilemma included: Does Sean know why Holly cannot decide whether or not to climb the tree? What will Holly's father think? Will he understand why if she does climb the tree?

Based on his extensive research, Selman proposed a five-stage model of the development of children's social cognitive under-standing, which he subsequently also applied specifically to children's understanding of friendship. As children's role-taking abilities improve so they are able to sustain increasingly sophisti-cated forms of friendship. Young, egocentric children at stage zero of social role-taking (about 3–6 years old) will see their friends simply as people who live nearby or are playmates. At stage one (approximately 6–8 years of age) children are able to recognise that their playmates have different emotions and intentions. A friend becomes anyone trying to do nice things for another. By stage two (roughly 8–10 years of age) children are starting to recognise that friendship implies a reciprocal relationship, sharing, mutual respect, kindness and affection. Preadolescents at stage three (about 10–12 years of age) have an awareness of the person-ality and preferences of their peers and a friend becomes a person with similar interests and values, someone with whom there is mutual support and the sharing of intimate, personal information. Finally, at stage four (approximately 12–15 years or older), the young adolescent is entering an era in which abstract possibilities feature. Relationships at this stage can show interdependence and intimacy and yet also a respect for the other's autonomy (Elbedour *et al.*, 1997). Paradoxically, the onset of the capacity to think in terms of abstract possibilities often produces another period of egocentrism in which other people are seen as being as concerned with the individual's attributes as is the individual him- or herself (Elkind, 1967). This may lead to heightened self-consciousness and an excessive concern about what others think. To many young adolescents, their spots and pimples may seem to be of as much interest and concern to other people as they are to themselves!

The general picture is of children's peer relationships becoming increasingly selective and other-centred with age, though Selman has been criticised for giving little consideration to the processes that drive these developmental changes (Schaffer, 1996). Certainly, a great many aspects of social and cognitive development are likely to be closely intertwined and mutually influencing. Positive peer relationships do seem to facilitate other aspects of social and cognitive development. For example, the free and open interaction of friends working together often means that they are able to solve problems more accurately, or solve more complex problems, than either of them could do individually (Azmitia and Montgomery, 1993). Similarly, children's role-taking skills do seem to be improved through playing or working with peers, especially friends (Nelson and Aboud, 1985). In interacting with peers rather than adults or older children, equal status allows differences in perspective and understanding to be aired and reconciled, giving insights into new possibilities and how these might be achieved.

Theories of mind

Closely related to the literature on role-taking is a line of cognitive developmental research examining children's intuitive awareness and ability to represent the mental states and internal psychological processes of others, i.e. their thoughts, memories, perceptions and emotional responses. This is an awareness of others as distinct psychological entities who may think and act differently to the way

45

the child itself would think and act. This broad area has been termed Theories of Mind (Moore, 1996). A theory of mind allows children to take the beliefs, expectations and goals of others into account as causes of behaviour as, hence, it enables them to function more effectively in their social world by permitting a more sophisticated explanation of the causes of observable events (Lalonde and Chandler, 1995).

The developmental origins of children's theories of mind are not yet clear, though there is ample evidence of such abilities from about 3 to 4 years onwards (Rice *et al.*, 1997). The precise age at which children first show evidence of a theory of mind is influenced by a number of factors, including the social experiences of the child. For example, children from large families appear to show theories of mind earlier than children from smaller families (Perner *et al.*, 1994). This is in accord with the finding that young children talk about their mental states more with siblings and peers than with their mothers (Brown *et al.*, 1996). In the two years after a child first exhibits a theory of mind, there are rapid and substantial increases in the accuracy and consistency of children's decisions and judgements which are based on this ability (Wellman and Banerjee, 1991).

Although the above discussion highlights the importance of a theory of mind for children in general, its impact and importance is most evident in children with autism. Although autistic children are socially responsive, they have difficulty with forming adequate social relationships because of major deficits in their interpersonal cognitive system (Sigman *et al.*, 1995). This is evident, for example, in their problems with co-ordinating their attention with that of another person. Similarly, autistic children seem to have problems with social referencing, the ability to use cues picked up from significant others to guide the construction of appropriate social responses to unexpected events. An interesting explanation that has been proposed for these relationship deficits has been in terms of the theories of mind approach. Autistic children appear to lack an understanding of other people's internal states and hence are unable to understand and predict their social actions.

Friendship concepts

In this section I will examine the developmental changes which occur in the content of children's friendship concepts. Although there is relatively little research on how relationship concepts affect actual patterns of interaction (Hartup, 1983), there is ample evidence suggesting that they do have major implications for the sorts of information that children are able to use as a basis for their relationships. Friendship concepts will determine what information is sought, attended to, how it is interpreted and the significance it is accorded. Friendship concepts will also determine the rules that are deemed to apply to the conduct of the relationship and the consequences which are appropriate to their violation (Bigelow *et al.*, 1992).

Various, often quite creative, methods have been used to access children's friendship concepts (see Erwin, 1993). Fortunately, the various diverse approaches that have been used have tended to produce fairly consistent patterns of results. I will outline just one influential study of children's friendship expectations that will serve as an example of this line of research. In their initial study, Bigelow and La Gaipa (1975) had schoolchildren of about 6 to 14 years of age write an essay about what is expected of a best friend that is different from other acquaintances. These essays were then divided into their constituent themes regarding friendship expectations. There was a clear pattern in the age at which friendship expectations of varying levels of complexity first consistently appeared. Based on Piaget's theory of cognitive development, Bigelow and La Gaipa proposed a three-stage model of the development of friendship expectations. Children were characterised as progressing from initially egocentric expectations through sociocentric and finally to empathic friendship expectations. The egocentric or situational stage lasts until about 7 or 8 years of age. The child at this stage is self-centred and concerned with his or her immediate situation. There is an emphasis on the concrete, external characteristics and behaviour of others. Friendship expectations at this stage emphasise rewards and costs, **propinquity**, shared activities, physical appearance, and possessions. Possession of an attractive toy or sweets is likely to be a great boost to the peer popularity of young children at this stage. Typical descriptive statements at this stage might be 'he plays football with me' or 'she lives near me'. Global dispositional and evaluative terms such as 'kind' or 'mean' are common, but are used as descriptions of recent behaviour rather than as insights into personality traits.

The sociocentric or normative stage lasts until about 11 years of age. The prime characteristic of this stage is an emphasis on sharing and the strict adherence to the rules and obligations of relationships. Friendship expectations are also starting to include a greater emphasis on psychological dimensions, on inner traits and qualities. Typical statements might include 'she shares more things', or 'he's big-headed'.

The empathic or internal-psychological stage of friendship expectations emphasises intimacy and trust, self-disclosure and the psychological characteristics of friends. The increasing differentiation and organisation of friendship expectations at this stage makes them extremely complex. Abstract psychological characteristics such as 'easy-going', 'generous', and 'someone you can talk to' can be attributed to others. The adolescent can comprehend and cope with inconsistencies and exceptions to the general characterisation of a person. Without too much effort the adolescent can accept that another can be both 'kind-hearted' and 'catty sometimes'.

An important point to note here is that the child's progression through these stages of friendship expectations does not imply that information important at a previous stage is subsequently ignored; rather, it is generally incorporated into and becomes but a part of a more sophisticated, complex friendship concept.

Friendship as a reciprocal relationship

Despite using very different research methods, though possibly because of their similar theoretical orientations, Bigelow and La Gaipa's work and that of Selman demonstrated encouragingly similar conclusions about children's understandings of friendship.

The major changes in friendship concepts can be explained in terms of the child's changing understanding of the nature of reciprocity within relationships (Youniss and Volpe, 1978).

In young children of 6 to 8 years old, reciprocity is simple and concrete. Children of this age emphasise the current material and social costs and benefits of an interaction; they know the actions necessary for friendship, such as sharing things and playing together, and see these in strict rule-based terms. Positive contributions will maintain relationships and negative contributions will lead to their collapse and dissolution unless appropriate patterns of behaviour are restored.

In the relationships of older children and preadolescents, the notion of reciprocity is extended to more specific activities and psychological characteristics. Relationships are seen as requiring the mutual accommodation of equal partners. The emphasis is moving to personal qualities rather than impersonal actions. Abstract qualities such as co-operation, intimacy, trust and mutual respect are sought in relationships, and the idea of the friend as an irreplaceable person is also beginning to emerge as a further form of reciprocity. In adolescence, reciprocity is further transformed to encompass a sense of shared identity. Trust and loyalty, support and the sharing of intimate secrets or problems becomes important. When such relationships are violated, the breach of trust and obligations must be acknowledged before they can be repaired.

Attributional processes

In the previous section I examined children's expectations of friendship. In this section I will examine the mechanism by which children infer these friendship qualities in others and anticipate the outcomes of their social interactions.

From the time of their birth children experience the co-occurrence of events and are encouraged to think in cause–effect terms. By 3 years of age they are well aware that people must be present to be the cause of an event, and that behaviour must precede an event to be its cause but, in their limited understanding, causality is based mainly on the associations that exist between events. The attributional error made by many preschoolers is to assume that most social behaviour is intentional. During the preschool and early primary school years children become increasingly proficient at distinguishing accidental from deliberate and involuntary acts. Although 5 and 6 year olds are quite able to make dispositional **attributions** to explain the behaviour of another, there is a tendency to focus on the immediate situation and external attributes at the expense of trait information. Their descriptions do not recognise or give weight to the idea that people will behave in a consistent manner in other situations (Rholes and Ruble, 1984). For young children, knowledge tends to be situation-specific and there is little recognition that a common base may underlie a variety of apparently very different behaviours in different situations. Thus a description such as 'nice' is likely to be used as a description of current behaviour rather than as a trait term which implies future conduct. The very limited attributional abilities of young children have severe implications for their ability to predict and manage the outcomes of their interactions. The consistent use of dispositional attributions does not appear until about 9 years of age, when simple trait terms such as 'nice' become a shorthand for expressing an expected consistency in another's patterns of behaviour. It is shortly after this attributional ability appears in common use that the close relationships of middle-childhood become possible.

Attributional 'biases' and social interaction

The picture presented so far has been of children as almost objective in their approach to processing social information. This is, of course, far from the full picture. In addition to the limits imposed by the individual's ability to process social information, at least two other factors are likely to influence the attribution process. First, the types of explanation which are considered appropriate to account for events will be influenced by cultural and sub-cultural factors. Some primitive cultures, for example, are more likely to accept explanations for some events or behaviour in terms of magic or witchcraft. Second, the situation in which we find ourselves may influence the pattern of our attributions. For example, children's attributions may be biased by their personal and social evaluations of others. Perceptions of a classmate's personality are likely to be affected by friendship and the classmate's popularity (Berndt and Das, 1987). These personal evaluations are also likely to have a very different impact depending on the behaviour or event being judged. A child will react very differently if tripped by a friend or by a disliked classmate. This is largely because of differences in the perceived intentions of the other child. In comparison to disliked peers, friends are generally seen as being more responsible for their positive behaviours, but less responsible and blameworthy for any negative behaviours (Waas and Honer, 1990). It is easy to see how these patterns of attribution can form the basis of self-sustaining reputations in children's peer groups. Especially for rejected children, these reputations may be an insurmountable obstacle to social acceptance. They may be at least part of the explanation for why so many social skills training programmes with rejected children seem to fail to produce long-term changes in their social status.

As well as the reputation of the other child, the social experience and popularity of the perceiver also affect how a social situation is interpreted. In a study by Earn and Sobol (1990), popular 10 to 12 year olds were more aware of the social cues and causes of behaviour and were more likely to see themselves as personally responsible for their social successes than were their less popular peers. Popular children were also more accurate in perceiving the effects of their behaviour and regarded their world as a more predictable, controllable place. These factors may be important contributors to the social confidence and success of popular children.

Social inadequacies and social failures may be internalised as negative self-perceptions (Boivin and Hymel, 1997), and a child's popularity does seem to be associated with characteristic patterns of coping with such problems. Whereas popular children may try to take into account complex factors, such as the motives of other people, when trying to explain their social failures, less popular children are more likely to explain their rejections in terms of persistent and uncontrollable factors, such as bad luck or personal incompetence. Because of this attributional style, rejected children may be prone to learned helplessness and patterns of thinking that exacerbate social maladjustment (Toner and Munro, 1996). The patterns of explanation of unpopular children may encourage them to believe that social success is a goal beyond their reach. Being able to explain social failure in terms of another's attitudes and behaviour, or simple incompatibility, can be a useful bolster to a child's **self-esteem**. Children not adopting this strategy may suffer severe consequences in terms of the assault on their self-esteem and debilitating self-attributions of personal incompetence which may feed through to a desperation and deterioration in their strategies for initiating relationships with others.

Summary

In this chapter I examined the cognitive bases of children's friendships. I focused on six closely related topics. First, I examined the development of a sense of Self or personal identity in the child. Only when the child is aware of a personal identity can there be an awareness of others also as separate entities. This lays the foundation for understanding others and the possibility of meaningful relationships. The topics of empathy, role-taking and theories of mind are concerned with the ability of children to metaphorically 'put themselves in the other person's shoes'. In terms of empathy, this is the ability to appreciate the emotional reactions of others. A primitive form of this ability is evident even in newborn children and this may provide the basic awareness of others on which more sophisticated role-taking abilities are built. Role-taking is the cognitive ability to see social situations from the other person's perspective. A theory of mind is the intuitive awareness of the psychological states of others. With an awareness of self and others the child can begin to establish personally meaningful relationships. Initially, these are relatively transient and merely sources of relatively immediate and concrete rewards. As the child's level of social cognitive understanding increases, so more sophisticated patterns of relationship can be envisaged and sought. Through childhood and into adolescence, friendship expectations become increasingly complex and focused on personality. Resulting from improvements in its attributional abilities, the child gradually becomes skilled at distinguishing the causes of another person's behaviour, and at determining if it was intended, was a result of the other's traits and dispositions, or merely an unintended accident of circumstances. However, the child is far from being an objective processor of information and the chapter concluded with an examination of some of the biases which can creep into the attribution process. It seems that attribution may often serve to reinforce the *status quo* and that social status may become relatively self-sustaining, with all the implications this potentially has for young children with poor social adjustment.

Further reading

Bukowski, W. M., Newcomb, A. F. and Hartup, W. W. (eds) (1996). *The company they keep: friendship in childhood and adolescence.* Cambridge: Cambridge University Press. Although I have included this book as suggested reading for this chapter, to greater or lesser degrees it contains material relevant to most of the chapters in this book. It also highlights the topics of current concern within the field of children's friendships. It contains good reviews of the literature up to about 1993, with a few references from 1994 and 1995. As with many edited books, the topics covered by the various chapters will probably provide you with far more information than you may need, though some topics may be lost in the gaps between the chapters.

Schaffer, H. R. (1996). *Social development.* Oxford: Blackwell. This is a very readable general textbook on social development that is packed with up-to-date detail. Many of the developmental phenomena covered in this chapter were dealt with relatively briefly and only from the point of view of their implications for children's peer friendships (e.g. the development of the sense of Self). The overview provided by this book will help to place children's friendships in a broader and more detailed developmental context and hence provide a more balanced account of their developmental significance.

Patterns
of social
interaction

I N CHAPTER 3, I EXAMINED HOW children's social cognitive abilities and social knowledge can affect their peer relationships, but we also need to know what children actually do in their relationships, and how they make use of their social knowledge to manage their relationships. In this chapter I will move the focus of attention to an examination of the impact of children's overt behaviour on their relationships. This is a crucial level of analysis as, if we exclude simple inferences based on physical appearance, the only insights that we have about a person's character and values are derived from their behaviour. However potentially attractive or compatible one child is to another, this has to be communicated if a relationship is to be established. And these behavioural cues are not, of course, only important at the early stages of a relationship. Different behaviours and different skills may be important at different stages of a relationship, but they will be important. However positive a child's intentions and attitudes are towards a friend, if these cannot be communicated or if wrong cues convey an incorrect message, misunderstandings and relationship difficulties are likely to ensue. On a positive note, an understanding of the interactional bases of children's peer relationships also has important implications for the possibility of **social skills training** to help isolated children, a topic explored further in Chapter 8.

This chapter examines some of the basic patterns of behaviour that promote successful peer interaction. First, I discuss the important distinction between popularity and friendship. I then move on to look at some broad patterns of verbal and non-verbal communication that underpin children's friendships and popularity. To make matters somewhat more specific and concrete, and to show the developmental changes that occur in patterns of relating, I outline typical patterns of interaction at several age ranges throughout childhood. As conflict, and its management, is a major factor in the success of relationships this is given specific, detailed attention. Within the broad patterns of relating that characterise children's friendships there exist a number of significant sex differences, and to give a balanced picture these also need to be taken into account. The final section of this chapter examines patterns of sex differences in children's friendships, the widespread sex segregation that characterises children's relationships, and the inevitable exceptions to the general rule, cross-sex relationships.

Popularity and friendship

It is important to note that a great many studies on children's peer relationships have examined what makes children popular, but this is not necessarily the same as what makes a good friend (Bukowski *et al.*, 1996). It is possible for a child to be popular with almost everyone and yet not feature as even one other child's 'best friend'. Similarly, many children may not be labelled popular but may well have stable, fulfilling relationships with one or a few close friends. In terms of later social adjustment, it seems that the possession of a close friend is more important than popularity. It is the child without a friend, the rejected social **isolate**, who seems most at risk for later social-adjustment and delinquency problems. Although much of the research on the relationship between social interaction and social status has simply tried to establish similarities and differences in patterns of behaviour between popular and unpopular children, some studies have attempted to determine whether these behaviours are actually a cause or consequence of popularity. It seems that it may be a little of both. The initial styles of interaction of unacquainted children are predictive of their later social status. Those most consistently positive and supportive towards their peers are likely to become the social stars and leaders (Shantz, 1986). Once social groups are established, these then also promote further social development. Being part of a group with other socially skilled individuals allows access to feedback which enables children to hone their skills still further. Meanwhile, the isolated, rejected child is likely to be involved in a cycle of frustrating, unsuccessful overtures to gain access to the popular cliques or else may give up and withdraw or be relegated into a group with other similarly excluded children. It is perhaps unfortunate that the children who would benefit most from being members of groups with socially skilled peers are the least likely to be admitted; popular and unpopular children appear to form distinct interactional groups that differ markedly in the pattern and quality of their interactions (Ladd, 1983).

Patterns of communication and interaction

In the course of interaction, verbal and non-verbal communication may serve important tactical functions, they are important both in attempts to initiate relationships and in regulating levels of intimacy. Even 3 and 4 year olds have been shown to use a more personal style of self-disclosure to friends than to non-friends (Rotenberg, 1995), and more communicatively skilled individuals seem more successful in establishing peer relationships (Kahen et al., 1994). The selectivity and significance of self-disclosure for promoting the development of a relationship becomes increasingly marked with age.

Non-verbal communication may be especially important in conveying emotional information, and hence important in social relationships. A number of studies have shown that non-verbal communication reflects and influences the levels of involvement and intimacy in children's peer relationships (Montemayor and Flannery, 1989). Non-verbal expressions of hostility may be especially significant determinants of rejection (Nowicki and Oxenford, 1989). Of course, the impact of non-verbal communication presupposes a sensitivity and ability to encode and decode such messages. Consequentially, children who possess these abilities have a decided social advantage over their less skilled peers. They are able to respond more appropriately and sensitively to others, making them highly desirable and popular as companions (Mendelson et al., 1994). Generally, older children are also more skilled communicators and this is reflected in the greater intimacy and stability that is possible in their friendships (Buhrmester and Furman, 1987).

A number of studies have outlined the characteristic patterns of behaviour that contribute to the social standing of children; these generally become increasingly complex and subtle with age. These patterns will now be described in terms of several rather arbitrary age blocks.

The first year

The importance of early peer interaction is becoming increasingly acknowledged, though many children without brothers and sisters may not experience such interaction on a regular basis until they enter day care or nursery school. Given the opportunity, social interest and attempts at peer interaction are evident from as early as 6 months of age, though non-social activity occupies much more of their time than does social behaviour in children of this age (Hartup, 1983). Young children of this age will look at each other, touch, imitate each other's actions, vocalise and smile at each other but lack the social skills to sustain social interaction sequences lasting more than a few seconds (Vandell et al., 1980). Already evident in these young children are the benefits of social experience with mothers, older siblings, or even just other peers. Infants with more extensive social experience tend to show more extensive and complex patterns of involvement with peers (Vandell and Wilson, 1987). Parents can make an important contribution to their young child's social development by ensuring that they have plenty of social opportunities and providing toys and materials that encourage interaction.

Two to five years

Throughout childhood there is a gradual shift to more interaction with peers and less with parents. The play of children becomes increasingly sophisticated and selective, and in it the beginnings of closer peer relationships and true friendship are evident. More

59

than half of all preschoolers establish relatively stable reciprocal friendships. By 4 years of age, children understand the concept of best friend and apply the term to select members of their peer group.

In their peer relationships skilled children are trying to be understood by friends and to respond to the needs of friends in a manner appropriate to the regulation of the encounter. Friends show more frequent, sustained interactions, connected discourse and speech relevant to fantasy and **role-play** activities than do strangers (Roopnarine, 1985). In general terms, peer preference and popularity at this age is associated with overall levels of giving and receiving positive, reinforcing behaviour, such as giving gifts, attention or acceptance (Snyder *et al.*, 1996). In contrast, less mature forms of play, negative behaviour such as aggression, non-compliance and the non-acceptance of others is associated with rejection (Pettit *et al.*, 1996). This does not imply that there is never any disagreement or conflict between friends. Some studies have shown similar levels of negative behaviour in friendship dyads and non-friendship dyads but, in the case of friends, this is balanced out by positive behaviours. Similarly, you may also have gathered from the above descriptions that rejected children are not necessarily socially withdrawn. Indeed, many studies have emphasised the importance of distinguishing between rejected and withdrawn children and have noted that rejected children may show levels of peer interaction on a par with their more popular counterparts. The difference is in the nature or quality of their interactions and in the reactions of other children to their social overtures. Preschoolers' perceptions of aggressive and co-operative behaviour in others are relatively salient and stable over a period of several weeks, and this is reflected in their actual behaviour and social status (Ladd and Mars, 1986).

The patterns of relationship behaviour discussed in the preceding paragraph set the stage for and are predictive of the child's social standing on entry to school (Ladd *et al.*, 1996). In an experimental study by Putallaz (1983), the interaction styles of preschoolers were assessed in the summer prior to beginning school. Subsequent social status when beginning school was predicted by the child's use of relevant conversation as a strategy to gain entry to social groups. This relationship was especially marked for children who also accurately interpreted the ongoing group behaviour. Children whose group entry gambits were disruptive or irrelevant to the ongoing activity were subsequently more likely to be rejected by their new schoolmates.

The primary school years

Peer relationships become increasingly important for children throughout their school years, and patterns of behaviour towards friends and non-friends become correspondingly and increasingly distinct. Reflecting developing social cognitive abilities, improvements in children's communication skills produce a reduction in their levels of aggressive behaviour and increases in positive interpersonal behaviours such as co-operation, compromise and sharing. These factors are closely related to children's social and friendship status.

Popular preschool and primary school-age children show increasing sensitivity and aptitude in their attempts to initiate interaction with others. They may initially 'hover' or play alongside an existing group, make supportive comments and provide constructive suggestions about ongoing activities (Ramsey and Lasquade, 1996). Conversations are more mutually oriented and complex and with a generally positive tone (Hartup and Stevens, 1997). Although less popular and rejected children often show just as many attempts at social interaction as their more popular counterparts, these are generally less well managed and show more inappropriate social behaviours. Generally, **neglected [status]** and **rejected [status]** children may appear self-centred, opinionated and perhaps bossy; they may violate the rules of games or even try to change the game being played. These entry attempts are characterised by other children as being disagreeable and are likely to lead to the child being rejected, ignored or, if accepted, to an interaction fraught with friction and disagreement. In the case of rejected children, there may even be overt physical aggression; popular children refrain from aggression. Unfortunately, many

FRIENDSHIP IN CHILDHOOD AND ADOLESCENCE

unpopular children see relatively few alternative strategies available to them; they are unable to understand the underlying reason or rule that has led to their rejection and hence are poor at generating alternative strategies for initiating peer contact (Stewart and Rubin, 1995). In sum, the early primary school years show a considerable continuity with the patterns of adaptation evident in preschoolers. Approach patterns and aggressiveness remain the crucial determinants of peer status.

Conflict management

A recurring theme in the literature on children's peer relationships is that aggressiveness is a major cause of social rejection. However, this conclusion has not gone without challenge. A particularly interesting study by Shantz (1986) statistically examined aggression and conflict as two separate factors. Conflict showed a much higher correlation with social rejection than did simple physical aggression. Learning to master conflict in personal relationships is a major task of childhood, and the open, honest relationships that exist between equals are a major training ground. Friends may be more critical of each other than non-friends but, especially as they get older, they are also more likely to explain and constructively discuss the bases of their disagreements (Dunn *et al.*, 1995). The child is learning the art of give and take, of compromise and how to defuse conflict. These are to become especially significant factors in the social status of older children.

Whereas 7 to 10 year olds may view support and conflict as being simple and exclusive opposites, by adolescence they are typically regarded as separate concerns. As such children are increasingly able to tolerate and accept conflict and not see it as necessitating the dissolution of a relationship (Parker and Gottman, 1989). With age, increasingly sophisticated strategies may be brought to bear to manage and resolve normal relationship conflicts.

Sex differences in patterns of relating

Although it varies in magnitude, it has been argued that sex segregation in children's relationships is a culturally universal phenomenon (Whiting and Edwards, 1988). The supposed reasons for this schism are qualitative differences in patterns of relating. Only a rudimentary understanding of the nature of gender is needed before children begin to acquire sex stereotypes and to show sex-typed behaviour and preferences for peers, toys and styles of play (Martin and Little, 1990). From about 2 years of age, girls are already beginning to show a social preference for approaching other girls; boys remain neutral a little longer but by 3 years of age also show a same-sex preference for playmates. Young girls increasingly show a relatively quiet, pro-social and co-operative style of behaviour in their play and social interactions. Young boys are more likely to be involved in an assertive, boisterous style of **rough and tumble play**. These are not particularly compatible patterns of interaction (Smith and Inder, 1993). For the young girl, interacting with boys can become marginalising, increasingly unpleasant and ineffective and so interaction is increasingly avoided. For both sexes, but most marked in young girls, there is a preference for same-sex peers and more sex-segregated social interactions. This initial segregation in patterns of play gives boys and girls a facilitative environment in which to fully develop their very different patterns of play and general social interaction skills (Braza et al., 1997). It also makes cross-sex interactions increasingly difficult.

By 5 years of age, boys are starting to show a stronger same-sex preference than girls and by middle-childhood the sex segregation in children's peer relationships is almost total. Perhaps in recognition of this, many activity groups of middle-childhood (such as Cubs and Brownies) are also sex-segregated. At this age boys are now likely to be the most derisive and rejecting of contact with the opposite sex. Girls' and boys' peer relationships now appear very different and have respectively been labelled as *intensive* and *extensive* (Waldrop and Halverson, 1975). The intensive relationships of girls are likely to focus on a single best friend and

63

are increasingly characterised by intimate conversation, personal knowledge of the friend and emotional involvement. In contrast, the relationships of boys are characterised as extensive because of their tendency to spend time mostly with a larger group of peers which may be fairly heterogeneous in terms of age and gathered together to engage in a specific task, game or activity.

Given the above descriptions of boys' and girls' relationships, it should come as no surprise to the reader that research is fairly consistent in finding both a developmental trend and a sex difference in the levels of intimacy associated with children's relationships. Female relationships are generally reported as showing higher levels of intimacy, sharing, trust and loyalty (Clark and Ayers, 1993), though different studies do vary in their reports of the size of these differences. This is not particularly surprising. As I will discuss in the next section, socialisation practices can markedly affect the degree to which children's relationships become sex-segregated. It would seem logical that levels of commitment and intimacy in relationships will mirror the way a relationship is organised no matter what the sex of the participants.

Although preadolescence does see a reduction in the degree of sex segregation of relationships as a romantic and sexual interest in the opposite sex starts to appear, it will take some years before a majority of adolescents will claim equal numbers of friends of both sexes rather than a majority of same-sex friends (Balding, 1993).

Socialisation of sex differences in relationships

From birth there are differences in the way baby boys and girls are treated that lay the foundations for the later differences in their patterns of relating to others. After about 6 months of age, girls are typically touched more, encouraged to stay closer to the mother, show more dependency, affectionate behaviour and expression of tender emotions. In contrast, boys are encouraged to participate in more active forms of play, often involving gross motor activities. As children become toddlers, parents are likely to seek playmates and companions of the same sex for them, supply them with sex-appropriate toys and encourage participation in sex-appropriate activities. Throughout childhood there is an emphasis from family, peers, schools and the media on the sex appropriateness of children's interests and behaviour. Continuing early patterns, greater independence and autonomy is encouraged in boys, who may be given more freedom to play with friends and allowed to range further away from the home and adult supervision; girls are likely to spend more of their leisure time in or close to the family and home (Coates, 1987).

Children forming groups is an almost inevitable part of growing up. Throughout childhood, peer groups become increasingly important to children. They give meaning to the child's world, contribute to a sense of personal identity, provide social rewards and generally are an essential part of the individual's socialisation. Unfortunately, these groupings may also directly contribute to the sex differences and sex segregation in children's relationships. The cognitive limitations of children, especially younger children, mean that these groups are almost inevitably going to be based on relatively superficial characteristics such as sex, regardless of adult pressures (Aboud, 1988).

With the formation of distinct peer groupings based on gender, a whole host of effects associated with group dynamics come into play. There is a tendency to minimise differences between members within a group and to maximise differences between members of different groups. Attributes irrelevant to the initial distinction are assimilated to the stereotype and 'boy' and 'girl' come to be seen as irreconcilable opposites. In comparison to out-group members, within-group characteristics are more valued, group members are perceived as more attractive and given preferential treatment. Out-group members, the opposite sex, are perceived as relatively homogeneous, less valued in terms of their personal characteristics and treated on the basis of their group membership.

Events in the child's world are likely to be interpreted in ways which bolster these group beliefs and reinforce group distinctions. There are also substantial pressures on children to behave in ways which will confirm group **norms**. Pressures to conform

65

increase with age until preadolescence, and violation of these peer expectations puts the child, especially boys, in severe risk of ridicule, exclusion from group activities and social rejection (Fine, 1987). As many parents have discovered to their chagrin, even against pre-existing patterns of behaviour and other agencies attempting to downplay sex differences in behaviour, the peer group is a powerful shaper of sex-typical behaviour in children (Fagot, 1981).

This general pattern of group dynamics makes it difficult for children to cross the boundaries of groups and behave in non-stereotypic ways. They are important contributors to sex prejudices, discrimination and segregation. So, can anything be done? It is to this question that I turn next.

Reducing sex segregation

Despite the pressures to sex segregation in children's relationships, research does indicate that such segregation can at the very least be markedly reduced. For example, to a large extent nursery schools often seem to reinforce the sex roles that are learnt early in life. In nursery schools where sex-typing is consciously avoided there is considerably less sex segregation in children's play (Bianchi and Bakeman, 1978). The specific role of the teacher is also important. Serbin *et al.* (1977) showed that with appropriate encouragement and reinforcement teachers could increase children's rates of co-operative cross-sex play from approximately 5 per cent of a child's time to almost 30 per cent. All the evidence points to the fact that with a little more thought and attention the institutional environment of pre-schools and schools could become a far richer context for learning about relationships.

Cross-sex relationships

The general sex segregation in children's relationships begins a gradual and consistent decline throughout the secondary school years, though examples of cross-sex relationships can be found at virtually all ages and specific social situations have been identified as increasing or decreasing the degree of sex segregation in children's interactions (Smith and Inder, 1990). For example, children are more likely to be involved in cross-sex interactions in the home neighbourhood than at school, or if they are involved in specific sports or activities which include both sexes and where there are few peers to witness the boundary violation. As a great deal of research on school-age children has been done in schools it is little wonder that sex segregation in peer relationships has traditionally been regarded as almost total. Modern methods of classroom organisation, emphasising co-operative interactions in small, mixed-sex instruction groups, does help to reduce **stereotyping** and produce an increase in integration (Lockheed, 1986), though very few children fully cross the gender divide. Of the few who do, most are girls and these individuals are typically labelled tomboys (Feiring and Lewis, 1989). These individuals will often fully participate in the adventurous play, fighting and teasing typical of boys' groups and seem to be fully accepted in this spirit. The outlook for boys who show stereotypically feminine interests and styles of behaviour is somewhat less sanguine: they risk being teased or ignored by both other boys and girls (Fagot, 1977). The experience of friendly interaction with peers of both sexes may be useful for both boys and girls. It provides them with the opportunity to encounter a wide range of behavioural styles and activities, reduces negative stereotyping of the opposite sex and increases the child's social opportunities. The better understanding and the skills in relating to others of the opposite sex that derive from children's experience of cross-sex interactions are likely to stand the child in good stead in his or her ability to establish satisfying relationships in later life.

Because of the pressures inhibiting cross-sex interactions in childhood, children show a number of ritualised mechanisms for enabling them to cope with the inevitable boundary violations that occur occasionally (Thorne, 1986). Some cross-sex interactions are deliberate but aim to strengthen gender boundaries, such as contests, chasing games or the common occurrence of boys invading and interfering with the games of girls. If girls seek access to boys' games, it is usually to join in rather than disrupt.

Despite their sex segregation, children's sex-role stereotypes make them well aware of each other as potential romantic partners. In late childhood, children may express an interest in others of the opposite sex, though not necessarily to the individuals concerned. Cross-sex interactions are typically strained and may only consist of indirect or overheard indications of attraction, teasing, and 'fooling around'. Sexual concerns may be cloaked in laughter, insults, and bravado (Fine, 1980). Perhaps because of this, early cross-sex relationships tend to be relatively unstable and transient. Nonetheless, by the time they are entering secondary school a few individuals begin to acknowledge cross-sex friendships and may even gain in social prestige on this count. Group discussions have the potential to cause embarrassment and so can arouse anxiety, but they can also provide support and reassurance. These patterns of interaction do not produce the relaxed, extended encounters necessary for friendship; the boundaries of same-sex groupings are only slowly crumbling, but the foundation has been laid upon which the cross-sex relationships of adolescence can be built. With the advent of the teenage years, cross-sex interactions and friendship choices become more realistic, and involve expectations of reciprocity on the part of the other person. Adolescent relationships are discussed in detail in Chapter 5.

Summary

After making the important distinction between popularity and friendship, I focused on two main themes in this chapter. First, the patterns of interaction that enable children to establish and manage relationships. Second, the behavioural characteristics underpinning the apparent sex segregation of peer relationships in middle childhood. Positive peer relationships are founded on a generally co-operative, pro-social approach to interactions. Of course, this orientation can only be imparted to others through verbal and non-verbal signals, so flexible, sensitive communication skills are paramount. Even if conflict does occur, with good communication skills this can be diffused and even become a valuable learning experience. Unpopular children often appear relatively egocentric, inflexible and possibly even aggressive in their interpersonal approaches. These are generally ineffective strategies that are frustrating for both participants. Aggression is one of the best predictors of social rejection in children. Within these general patterns of social behaviour there are distinct sex differences in children's styles of relating. These make cross-sex encounters potentially unpleasant and relationships difficult. By middle-childhood there is an almost complete sex segregation in children's peer relationships. This is partly a natural product of cognitive development, partly the result of situational factors which promote sex segregation and partly the result of group dynamics and conformity effects. Throughout childhood and approaching adolescence, children evolve a number of strategies for managing occasional cross-sex encounters. These provide a means of diffusing boundary violations in young children but also ultimately provide the foundation on which the cross-sex relationships of adolescence may be built.

Further reading

Canary, D. J., Cupach, W. R. and Messman, S. J. (1995). *Relationship conflict*. London: Sage. As mentioned in this chapter, conflict, and how it is managed, is a major issue in children's relationships. This textbook provides a detailed, readable overview of the general topic of conflict. It covers both adults and children, a variety of relationships and a basic introduction to research methods in the area.

Newcomb, A. F. and Bagwell, C. L. (1995). Children's friendship relations: A meta-analytic review. *Psychological Bulletin*, 117, 306–47. This paper looks in more detail at a major theme of this chapter, that characteristic patterns of interaction underpin successful friendships. A sophisticated statistical analysis of eighty-two existing studies on children's friendships was used to draw out the pattern differences between friends and non-friends. The impact of other variables, such as age of participants, the strength of the relationship and research methodologies, was also examined. Not an easy paper to read, but worth the effort.

Chapter 5

Adolescence

THE ADOLESCENT YEARS HAVE TRADITIONALLY been treated (and still are by many authors) as an area of interest distinct from the rest of childhood. Relationships during this era have often been examined as entities separate from and largely discontinuous with those that went before, despite 'the glaring obvious proposition that the groundwork for transition in adolescence must have been laid in childhood' (Coleman, 1995). I have included a chapter on adolescence in this book as my small contribution to the growing trend to break down this barrier and in an attempt to provide a more complete, balanced and integrated view of friendships throughout the pre-adult years.

The advent of adolescence

The entry to adolescence is a time of dramatic changes. The child is changing physically with the onset of puberty, psychologically as more abstract patterns of thinking are developed, and socially in terms of new roles, new patterns of relating and becoming a part of the prevailing youth culture. This time of great changes has been characterised as a time of great psychological turmoil and social upheaval for adolescents, a time when they rebel against the adult and family values that were imposed on them throughout childhood. In fact, in most cases this picture is an over-exaggeration and most adolescents are remarkably level-headed and able to resolve any developmental problems they may encounter (Kirchler *et al.*, 1995).

In adolescence, there is a growing ability and preoccupation with achieving intimacy in relationships and yet closeness can be difficult to achieve. This situation is especially marked in the newly emerging cross-sex relationships of young adolescents, which can be uncomfortable to the point of antagonistic. Throughout adolescence there is a continuing shift in the balance of time spent in interaction with parents and peers. Interaction with peers becomes increasingly significant and they gradually become the major reference group when making decisions and evaluations concerning current activities and events. Intimacy with peers and parents increases throughout adolescence (Rice and Mulkeen, 1995), though the balance in this pattern does change. As adolescence progresses, and somewhat earlier for boys than girls, peers gradually overtake parents as the adolescent's major source of intimacy and social support (Frey and Rothlisberger, 1996). Interactions with parents become increasingly concerned with routine matters such as the management of time and behaviour (Smetana and Asquith, 1994). In early to mid-adolescence, this role often puts parents in the position of placing prohibitions and restrictions on the young adolescent's activities, such as how late they may stay out in the evening, and as such is a common source of conflict and friction within the family. Despite these occasional disputes and disagreements, parental and peer group values are not necessarily opposed. The peer group, typically composed of adolescents from similar social backgrounds, is often a powerful force in support of many of the fundamental attitudes and values held by parents. The level of influence on the adolescent of the peer group relative to the family is likely to depend on a number of personal and situational factors. It is certainly more significant for adolescents who perceive a lack of adequate parental support. In families disrupted by divorce or other events, friends, and the peer group generally, can become an important point of reference for the adolescent.

Despite the above qualifiers, providing parents are not rejecting or indifferent to their child, throughout adolescence most individuals will still regard their parents as their major sources of support and self-esteem while attempting to resolve the many new and conflicting demands that they are experiencing. Relationships with parents may remain especially important at times of transition, such as when beginning a new school or college.

Thinking about relationships

With the sophisticated, abstract patterns of thought that are starting to be displayed as children enter adolescence, some individuals experience a period of egocentrism in which they are excessively concerned with themselves as a centre of other people's attention and evaluation (Elkind, 1978). They become intensely concerned about their own needs, social attributes and relationships. How do they look? Do other people regard them as attractive? What are their relationship prospects? What is their social standing relative to their peers? This excessive self-consciousness peaks at about 12 to 14 years of age and then declines gradually. It is a major cause for a parallel pattern of shyness which is also typical of late childhood and adolescence.

In the remainder of this section I will examine two topics which derive their significance from the part they play in helping adolescents on their voyage of self-exploration. First, physical appearance and attractiveness. The physical changes of puberty, the excessive self-consciousness of early adolescence and a growing interest in the opposite sex often combine to create major concerns about how others evaluate the adolescent's physical appearance and attractiveness. The second major issue that I will examine in this section is the role of similarity in adolescent relationships. Similarity provides self-affirmation to the adolescent, indicates a likelihood of social acceptance and provides a foundation on which relationships may be built. I will now examine in more detail each of these topics in turn.

Physical appearance

Because of the physical changes that occur during adolescence, coming to terms with one's body and appearance has been regarded as a major developmental task of this phase of development (Erikson, 1963). The adolescent is likely to be intensely aware of, and attach great importance to, their own and other people's physical appearance. Physical appearance is a major component of the adolescent self-concept, and the self-fulfilling stereotypic expectations of others may have important implications for the adolescent's social opportunities and adaptation (Perkins and Lerner, 1995). Physically attractive individuals, especially girls, have a decided social advantage over their less attractive counterparts. For example, they are more likely to have, and gain the kudos from having, a steady dating partner (Chess et al., 1976).

Physique and body image are major concerns of many adolescents. Being over- or underweight can substantially impact on the adolescent's self-image and affect their social opportunities (Coleman and Hendry, 1990). The importance and consequences of physical attractiveness may be greater for girls than boys because it is a more significant part of the feminine gender role and self-concept in many cultures (Freedman, 1984). The more intimate relationships of girls also enable them to engage in a more detailed analysis and evaluation of their relative standing on attributes such as physical attractiveness (Felson, 1985). For some adolescent girls, an attractive appearance is so central to the feminine sex role that this may cause severe adjustment problems, including a negative body image, eating disorders, self-consciousness, feelings of low self-esteem and withdrawal (Freedman, 1984). Paradoxically, these adjustment problems may be greater for more rather than less attractive individuals as their appearance is often a more significant component of their self-esteem (Zakin et al., 1984).

Similarity

The multitude of changes in the lives of adolescents prompt a strong need for the consensual validation provided by similar peers. Similarity tends to occur on many levels. At the simplest level, adolescent friends are likely to be similar on a number of basic personal and demographic characteristics such as age, sex, race and educational background. Of course, many of these similarities are probably general characteristics of the peers that the individual most commonly encounters. They are likely to go to the same class in the same school in the same neighbourhood.

75

Nonetheless, even within the broad field of eligibles there is generally a selection of more rather than less similar others as friends (Clark and Ayers, 1992).

There is also a similarity of same- and opposite-sex friends in terms of levels of physical attractiveness. This is often termed the matching hypothesis. Fairly early in their lives individuals realise their level of attractiveness, the value this has in social relationships, and the likelihood of rejection if they approach others of substantially greater levels of attractiveness than themselves. As well as the implicit reward-value of physical appearance, there is an associated stereotype. Similar levels of attractiveness may be used as a cue that the other person is also likely to hold similar attitudes and important aspects of personality (Erwin and Calev, 1984), factors which other research has shown to be important bases of relationships.

As relationships progress, other deeper levels of actual similarity are likely to become important. These include important personal attitudes, such as school orientation, music, fashion, drugs usage, personal needs and aspects of personality (Gavin and Furman, 1996). Aspects of attitudinal similarity may become broader and deeper as relationships develop. The participants in friendships that survive throughout a school year actually grow to be more similar to each other as they jointly develop some new interests and take on some of the existing characteristics of their friends (Kandel, 1978). As relationships develop there are notable sex differences in the types of similarity that are important. From mid-adolescence girls begin to show an emphasis on similarity of psychological traits while boys emphasise similarity in terms of activities and patterns of interaction. In late adolescence both also show a return to an emphasis on the perceived physical characteristics of others (Duck, 1975), possibly reflecting the increasing significance of cross-sex relationships. Overall, these changes reflect the increasing use of abstract interpersonal descriptions, sex differences in patterns of relating, and the process of coming to terms with physical maturation.

In addition to providing the consensual validation of an adolescent's attitudes, values and behaviour, similarity can also serve important functions in terms of group dynamics. Similarity can function as an expression of solidarity and conformity within the supremely important friendship group. Little surprise then that similarity appears to be a consequence as much as a cause of adolescent friendships and is highly valued within the broader friendship group.

Cliques and crowds

As they enter adolescence children are leaving behind them much of the dependency on parents and other adults that characterised their earlier years, but they are still denied the full autonomy of adulthood. In their peer groups they can to a large extent develop their own culture and rituals and assert their independence of adult values and rules. These peer groups, and the close friendships within the context of these broader groups, are important in helping the adolescent clarify their sense of personal identity as they become increasingly independent of their parents, provide them with social status and ultimately permit the development of cross-sex relationships (Giordano, 1995). As is evident from this description, the quality of relationship that the adolescent is able to establish with the peer group is important. To the extent that individuals can identify and integrate with a group they will derive corresponding benefits in terms of the amount of emotional support, assistance and social learning that is possible, and this in turn is likely to be reflected in their self-esteem (Kirchler et al., 1995).

A notable feature of the peer network as the child enters adolescence is its increase in size and complexity. Peer relationships begin to extend beyond the dyad or small clique of friends to a larger, more loosely knit group, often termed a crowd, consisting of several cliques that regularly associate in the school or home neighbourhood (Urberg et al., 1995). These groups are typically of similar or admired individuals (in terms of age, sex, class, leisure interests, etc.) and become the focus for the adolescent's social activity (Csikszentmihalyi and Larson, 1984).

77

It becomes increasingly important to the individual to be accepted and positively evaluated by their wider peer group and so new skills are required to cope with this changing and expanding social world.

Many venues may serve as meeting points for adolescent groups. Popular modern venues are shopping malls and amusement arcades, though a street corner, park or other convenient assembly point may also serve this function (Fisher, 1995). A large amount of the adolescent's free time is spent in cliques and crowds, discussing such topics of major interest as the activities of other members of the group, aspects of popular culture, such as the latest fashions, recent record and film releases, and television programmes. Adolescents report spending more time simply talking to friends than in any other activity. Involving much 'fooling around' and laughter this activity, that may seem aimless and pointless to an outsider, is seen as amongst the most fulfilling of their activities by the adolescents themselves (Csikszentmihalyi *et al.*, 1977).

Despite the significance of the peer group for adolescents, they still spend more of their time alone than with peers. Adolescents also spend a substantial amount of time considering their relationships and identity (Csikszentmihalyi and Larson, 1984) and, perhaps because of the centrality of the group in the adolescents' life, this is also a time when loneliness is a common experience.

Pressures to conform

The benefits that accrue to the individual as a result of being part of a group can produce powerful pressures to conform to group norms. For new members, this may be increased through initiation rites and tests of loyalty, both of which serve to strengthen group cohesion (Moreland and Levine, 1982). The pressures to conform are likely to be most marked in relation to matters concerned with the activities and management of the group itself, such as spending time with the group and adhering to group norms (Brown, 1982). Significant deviations are likely to bring the individual to the focus of group attention with a consequent increase in the pressures to come into line. Failure to do so may lead to marginalisation within the group or even, ultimately, to exclusion.

Although some adolescent groups can undoubtedly serve to support and sustain delinquent and antisocial behaviour, their significance for most adolescents is frequently over-estimated (Kirchler *et al.*, 1995), especially by worried parents! Contrary to popular belief, in many areas of concern, such as sexual behaviour and drug use, the normative pressures from the group may be substantially less than for many other activities. Indeed, in early adolescence at least, the pressures may often be against these activities and overall may be more positive than negative (Berndt and Zook, 1993). It appears that when significant pressures to engage in activities such as drinking, sex and drug use do start to feature in later adolescence, this may largely be a case of coming into line with adult values and norms of behaviour rather than teenage rebellion.

Conformity to the adolescent peer group appears to peak in the early teens and then gradually decline. This pattern has been explained as resulting from the individual's increasing romantic interests, which moves the focus of their social attention outside of the group. It is equally feasible to explain this decline in terms of the general reduction in levels of conformity in later adolescence (Durkin, 1995), or because older adolescents have clarified their sense of identity, social roles and social status, and thus are less dependent on the affirmation and support of the peer group. As adolescence progresses, the costs of conformity begin to outweigh the status benefits that are conferred, and the social opportunities in dyads and small friendship groups outside of the crowd begin to exceed those within the broader crowd structure (Brown *et al.*, 1986). The importance of the crowd for the individual gradually declines over the teenage years.

Friendship in adolescence

Throughout adolescence, both sexes rate their same-sex friendships as more important than their cross-sex relationships (Lempers and Clark-Lempers, 1993), perhaps reflecting the fact that these relationships may have been established longer and occupy a much greater and more diverse part of the individual's social life. Though less absolute, the sex cleavage that was so characteristic of the relationships of middle-childhood is still evident as the child enters adolescence (Douvan and Adelson, 1966). There remains a substantial segregation in the social relationships of adolescents throughout the high-school years, only diminishing in strength in late adolescence (Montemayor and Van Komen, 1985). Nonetheless, the form and function of this sex schism in relationships is changing to reflect the different **gender role** stereotypes and intimacy needs of adolescents.

Patterns of intimacy and stability

Friendships appear relatively stable in adolescence (Claes, 1992), reflecting the adolescent's more stable interests, better cognitive abilities, and a capacity to constructively handle any conflicts that may arise. However, if such a relationship does break down it will be experienced as a substantial loss and will be difficult to replace. The irreplaceability of adolescent relationships is due in part to the investment of time and effort that has gone into close relationships at this age, and partly because the field of eligible replacements is itself likely to be severely limited due to the existing social and friendship commitments of the adolescent's peers. The end result is that the size of friendship networks shows relatively little change in adolescence (Berndt and Hoyle, 1985).

A number of studies have reported sex differences in the patterns of intimacy in adolescence which are a natural continuation of those observed in younger children. For adolescents generally, the best friend is seen as a constant companion and a relatively irreplaceable confidant. Intimacy is a matter of degree rather than an absolute difference between the sexes, and dimensions such as emotional support and helping, acceptance and genuineness seem to be equally stressed by both sexes (Bigelow and La Gaipa, 1980).

In comparison with males, adolescent females are more concerned with forming emotional, intimate relationships with just one or a few best friends (Jones and Costin, 1995). Nonetheless, they do not differ markedly from boys in the actual number of friends they possess. For adolescent girls, the larger group is seen primarily as a network of intimate friendships, a place to find a friend, and a source of support and confidences. Adolescent girls depend heavily on their friends as confidantes through whom they can come to understand themselves and their place in a rapidly expanding social world. In comparison with adolescent boys, girls rate their friendships as higher in affection, intimacy, companionship and satisfaction (Jones and Costin, 1995). Adolescent girls are more likely to turn to the broader peer group for support than are boys but, unlike boys, do not generally feel a sense of group allegiance or that they are bound by a set of group rules (Douvan and Adelson, 1966). Adolescent girls invest much more in their close personal relationships rather than in the broader friendship group. They are in more frequent contact with and are more likely to possess an intimate knowledge of their close friends than are boys (Belle, 1989). With this knowledge comes a great stress on the importance of trust and confidentiality. Violation of this trust is a common cause of conflict in relationships, though increasingly sophisticated methods of conflict resolution are being developed throughout adolescence. Rather than intransigence, demands and threats or appeals to authority, there is an increasing ability to seek constructive solutions through negotiation and the generation of alternatives that might create a consensus (Leyva and Furth, 1986). Much of this is possible because of the open and sophisticated patterns of communication that characterise positive adolescent relationships. In relationships which have an in-built imbalance of power, such as those with parents and teachers, such open, sophisticated approaches to resolving problems are considerably less likely.

sex friendships hit a particularly difficult phase for girls between the ages of about 14 and 16 years. Girls are extremely demanding in their need for similarity and reciprocity with their friends. The value they attach to such characteristics is evident in their concomitant demands for absolute loyalty and commitment. Even if romantic relationships are formed, their intimacy and importance are unlikely to rival that of the relationship with the best friend (Lempers and Clark-Lempers, 1993). This pattern may be even more marked for adolescent boys, whose relationships generally appear to be characterised by lower levels of intimacy than those of girls of the same age (Werebe, 1987). The heavy demands on friendships at this age can prove costly. For mid-adolescent girls, a relationship partner's excessive demands or shortcomings may produce conflict and levels of relationship dissolution in excess of those found in the cooler friendships of adolescent males of the same age (Parker and Gottman, 1989). Broken relationships are a particularly serious occurrence at this age as most other potential partners will themselves already be involved in other established and equally jealously guarded relationships.

Adolescent boys' close friendships are closely tied into the broader social crowd or gang (Eder and Hallinan, 1978). In their larger groups, boys evolve and learn to live within a complex organisational structure with a broad system of rules and possibly including a number of individuals who are not particularly liked. The group members as a whole are an important source of support, identification and vicarious learning for the adolescent male in his move towards personal autonomy and independence from the family and other sources of authority. The costs of this support are the obligations of loyalty and conformity to group rules and norms that are demanded.

Although adolescent males do show intimacy in their self-disclosures to friends, to a large extent their relationships are based on common interests and activities, enjoyable companionship and similarity of attitudes. There is less interest in a deep and repeated analysis of personal experience and reactions that are so characteristic of adolescent girls' friendships (Dolgin and Kim, 1994).

The emergence of cross-sex relationships

Children's knowledge of gender-role stereotypes makes them intensely aware of each other as potential romantic partners, but they nonetheless generally follow a pattern of avoiding cross-sex contact apart from some ritualised interactions. Through elementary school and increasing with age, cross-sex interaction is risky in school. Though some cross-sex interaction does occur under other circumstances, such as in the home neighbourhood or at church, these contacts are often hidden or downplayed in the tightly knit peer groups at school (Thorne, 1986).

Perhaps the most distinctive feature of adolescent relationships is the breakdown in the publicly displayed sex segregation that was so typical of childhood. Although there is still a good deal of teasing initially, and this does not allow the relaxed, extended interactions necessary for friendship, adolescence does see a progression towards a more balanced social network and the establishment of cross-sex friendships and romantic relationships (Balding, 1993). Mirroring earlier social patterns, these changes do not necessarily occur evenly in the adolescent's social world. Groups outside the school are likely to become smaller and of mixed sex much more rapidly than those within school (Montemayor and Van Komen, 1985).

A number of studies have examined the emergence of cross-sex relationships in adolescence. A classic study by Dunphy (1963) outlined five main stages in the process of transition from the single-sex groups and friendships of childhood to the mixed groups and cross-sex relationships of adolescence. The starting point of the process, stage 1, is the pre-crowd, represented by the friendship cliques of late childhood. These are groups typically consisting of four to six same-sex friends. An important point to note here is that the individual members of these cliques are not necessarily all close friends with each other. Similarly, members of a clique may still have close friends that are outside of that group (Urberg *et al.*, 1995). Cliques may also differ in their exclusivity. Although the boundaries between cliques are seldom clearcut, they can differ substantially in their accessibility to outsiders (Cotterell, 1996).

Some may be relatively fixed and resist the entry of outsiders not already associated with the group or one of its existing members in some way; others may be relatively open and fluid in their composition (Zisman and Wilson, 1992). Closeknit cliques may have grown out of earlier childhood friendship networks and be based around friends who live in the same neighbourhood and have known each other and shared activities and interests for many years. Exclusivity may also reflect the status of a clique, with higher status cliques being less accessible. Paradoxically, this may lead such cliques to be both highly attractive because of the social advantages they offer and yet derided for their exclusivity and air of superiority. Some of the more fluid cliques may be largely associations of convenience, characteristic of such places as school cafeterias or activity clubs.

Each clique is relatively independent and often organised around leaders who possess admired traits or abilities (Adler and Adler, 1995). Most cliques are likely to have at least two leaders: a social leader who models appropriate interpersonal behaviour, and especially behaviour towards the opposite sex, and a task leader who is concerned with the more general day-to-day running of the group. Other clique members may temporarily take on the mantle of leadership if they possess expertise in some task or activity, such as a sport or game. The task leader is likely to be the major force in deciding group membership, activities and enforcing norms. Enforcing norms need not entail coercion on the part of the group. It can be an extremely subtle process. Offering help in important areas but not unimportant areas, modelling appropriate behaviour, or simply jointly discussing and evolving the social norms of the group may serve to promote uniformity. Throughout most of adolescence these relatively close groups will provide the personal, intimate support of individual members within the wider social milieu. The preadolescents in these elementary groups may be highly aware of and interested in members of the opposite sex but their opportunities and involvement in cross-sex interactions are limited, tentative and often involve a great deal of friction.

With the advent of the early adolescent years comes Dunphy's second stage in the development of cross-sex relationships: the beginning of the crowd. This is marked by same-sex cliques beginning group-to-group interaction. These group inter- actions form the basis for the third stage: the crowd in transition. This stage is characterised by the emergence of the mixed-sex adolescent crowd. This still consists of mostly unisexual cliques, though a few individuals begin to affirm rather than avoid charges of cross-sex friendships and there is often even a gain in status by publicly choosing a companion of the opposite sex. Gradually, mixed-sex cliques also begin to appear within the crowd, particularly among the leaders and high-status members. These individuals may also start dating one another. These patterns of interaction provide important sources from which the less socially advanced members of the group can learn.

Gradually, by mid- to late-adolescence, the mixed-sex cliques begin to replace the same-sex cliques, and opposite-sex peers are starting to assume importance as companions (Buhrmester and Furman, 1987). This takes us to stage four, which is the fully developed crowd, consisting of several mixed-sex cliques in close association. Adolescent crowds are a common sight around many streets, parks or other public places and represent an important place for the sexes to meet. Older adolescents and those seeking dates may make more use of these busy social meeting places. Conversely, those feeling threatened or frustrated in their hopes of romantic relationships may retreat from such places of high exposure (Silbereisen et al., 1992). The crowd stage often occurs somewhat later for boys than girls, perhaps reflecting, at least in part, their greater difficulty in coping with and adapting to the more intimate, personal style of interaction that characterises relationships with and among adolescent girls (Dunphy, 1972). Initially, these new mixed-sex cliques continue to interact with each other in large crowd activity, though this gradually declines as couples start to form more serious relationships. In stage 5, the crowd begins to disintegrate and fragment, leaving groups of loosely associated couples. Although this original research was conducted some considerable time ago, the general pattern of adolescent peer relationships outlined above has continued to receive support from more recent studies (e.g. Urberg et al., 1995).

Summary

This chapter examines how childhood relationships change as the individual enters and progresses through adolescence. Adolescence is a critical period of physical, psychological and social change for the individual. Changes in physical appearance highlight this as a major area of awareness and concern for many adolescents, and an important factor in their relationships. Similarity on a number of personal and social attributes is also sought in order to provide consensual validation and a sense of group identity for the individual during these times of uncertainty and change. Same-sex friendships become more intimate and irreplaceable throughout adolescence, and generally demand higher levels of loyalty and commitment. This is especially marked in female relationships. Despite being a period of many changes, undoubtedly the most notable feature of adolescence is the development of cross-sex relationships. The sex schism that was so prominent a feature of children's relationships begins to break down. Groups of same-sex peers begin to interact with other groups of peers of the opposite sex. Gradually, mixed-sex groups emerge and out of these come mixed-sex couples.

Further reading

Cotterell, J. (1996). *Social networks and social influences in adolescence.* London: Routledge. Up to date and very readable. The emphasis is very definitely on social networks, and as such this book provides an outline of the broader social setting within which adolescent friendships are played out. It gives relatively little attention to other close peer relationships (such as romantic relationships).

Jackson, S. and Rodriguez-Tomé, H. (eds) (1995). *Adolescence and its social worlds.* Hove: Erlbaum. This covers a broader range of topics and in more detail than Cotterell, though it can be heavier going in places. In many ways the two texts complement each other quite well. As well as friendship, this text examines a variety of other relationships (e.g. dating and relationships with grandparents) and related issues such as research methods, loneliness and stress.

Chapter 6

Relationships
in context

I N THE PRECEDING CHAPTERS of this book I have focused on how children's friendships vary with age. In the main, friendships were treated as if they were relatively homogeneous. Even the most casual recollection by anyone of the variety of their relationships will confirm that this is self-evidently not the case. A relationship does not exist in isolation, it exists in the context of a multitude of other factors which will affect how it is to be played out. On a number of occasions I did touch on examples and topics that clearly indicated the potential variety of influences on the form and function of children's friendships, and the aim of this chapter is to broaden and deepen these considerations. Under the heading of 'context' I will gather together a very broad range of factors that may affect the pattern of children's friendships either directly, through their impact on the relationship itself, or indirectly, through their influence on the individual participants.

All friendships have a history, are located in a given economic, geographic, cultural and historical setting, are influenced by a variety of other social institutions, and each is but a part of the individual's broader relationship network. Relationships, and social behaviour more generally, are both constructed from and contribute to the broader social context in which they occur. To represent this reciprocal pattern of influence, ecological psychologists argue that there is a tendency for behaviour and environment to become similar in form, summarised in the term 'synomorphy'. In other words, in a dynamic process of mutual influence the environment and the person are mutually changed until they reach a point where there is an equilibrium between the two forces. In this chapter I will examine both how children's relationships are influenced by the context in which they occur and also how children may choose specific contexts in which to play out their relationships. Specifically, I will examine cross-cultural differences in patterns of relating, some characteristics of families that impact on relationships, how the home neighbourhood, preschools and schools may limit and direct children's styles of relating to their peers, and how children's toys may promote specific styles of play and interaction.

Cross-cultural perspectives

The drive to form relationships is a universal phenomenon, though the form, expectations and obligations of such relationships may vary significantly from one culture to another. Friendships are not simply influenced by the culture in which they occur, they are an integral part of the collective interpretation and reproduction of that culture (Corsaro, 1994). Western culture, with its emphasis on individualism and freedom of choice, gives considerable significance to intimate personal relationships. Many other cultures give considerably less emphasis to personal relationships than they do to other ties such as kinship and the relationships between community members (Harrison et al., 1995). Indeed, in many cultures personal relationships are largely determined or limited by a person's family, caste or membership of various social groups (Guddykunst et al., 1996).

The economic foundations of a society determine patterns of family life and social interaction. These in turn affect children's patterns of peer relationships. The very different lifestyles of hunter-gatherers, nomadic herdsmen, isolated farmers and individuals in urbanised industrial societies have a major impact on children's group sizes and consequently the opportunities they have to meet and interact with peers. Many of the patterns of relating we now take for granted are, in fact, a product of the relatively recent industrialisation and urbanisation of Western society with its attendant impact on family and community structures. In particular, Western culture and, especially, the education system do often seem to promote and institutionalise age and sex schisms in children's activities and groupings from a relatively early age (Montemayor and Van Komen, 1985). In smaller and more isolated communities such a dividing of children into subgroups may not be feasible or considered desirable. In some cultures the limited number of other children in a given social group may mean that even the opportunity for peer interaction is limited. In these situations, many of a child's interactions are likely to be with parents, other adults or relatives and children of quite a wide variety of ages. In this sort of group the older children may even take on some of the responsibilities for the care and socialisation of younger group members (Whiting and Edwards, 1988).

So far this discussion has been at the large-scale level of cross-cultural comparisons. In the following sections I will begin an examination of relationships in a variety of settings within the Western cultural context.

The role of the family

Parents set the stage upon which the friendships of their children are played out, though their effect is likely to depend on the age of the child. The impact of parents on relationships is likely to be most marked with younger children because of their greater dependence. Preschoolers may be almost totally dependent on their parents for opportunities to meet their peers. Parents who make the effort to establish opportunities for peer contact for their young children are doing them a great service as these early foundations are a crucial base for the socialisation of children into their peer group. Such fortunate children are likely to develop a large number of different play partners, more consistent companions outside of school and greater peer acceptance (Ladd and Golter, 1988). Adolescents have considerably more independence in their peer relationships than do younger children. Nonetheless, as they strive to assert their autonomy from the relatively few controls that are exerted by parents, this may in itself be a cause of relationship difficulties and conflict.

Social class and poverty

Social class and family finances are major factors affecting the child's experience of family life. At the simplest level, family income is likely to be a major determinant of the type of accommodation that can be afforded. Poorer families are likely to be larger and to live in poorer, more crowded conditions with fewer opportunities for privacy. Although it is difficult to separate out the effects of overcrowding from other factors, such as the quality of housing, it does appear that the forced interaction in such overcrowded conditions may have deleterious consequences. Far from promoting social skills, positive social interaction, and relationships, it may result in social withdrawal or aggressiveness towards peers (Murray, 1974).

The impact of social class extends considerably beyond the effects of associated differences in the physical environment. Social values and beliefs impact on the socialisation practices of parents and are reflected in their children's social behaviour and friendship expectations. Restrictive, authoritarian styles of child control and the use of physical punishment is more likely in families of low socio-economic status. Through **modelling** and **reinforcement** this is likely to promote more aggressive and generally more physical styles of interaction in children (Parke and Slaby, 1983). Research does suggest that verbal interactions may be a more important foundation for relationships in children from a middle-income background and physical interactions may be more important in children from low-income families. Children may even come to find the style of interaction of other children from different socio-economic backgrounds aversive (Gottman *et al.*, 1975). This is a potentially important point for social educators who wish children from different social backgrounds to work together, and for psychologists contemplating social skills training with children from different socio-economic backgrounds.

Social class also has an indirect effect on children's relationships because of its impact on their use of community organisations and social facilities, such as youth clubs, the Cubs and Brownies. Involvement in the community is important because it provides children with an approved meeting-ground, a place to make friends and acquire and test new social skills. Children's involvement in community organisations generally increases with age until about adolescence, though individuals from higher socio-economic backgrounds are more encouraged and more than twice as likely to actually participate in them. Often their mothers will also become involved in supporting the activity. Children from lower socio-economic backgrounds are more likely to use community facilities only on an *ad hoc* basis or if they are specifically targeted at them (O'Donnell and Stueve, 1983).

The community environment

One very direct way in which the community environment affects children's peer relationships is through its effect on the physical proximity between individuals. One consequence of proximity is that it may lead to regular contact or exposure to the other person. The child's attitude towards the other may then be influenced by a **mere exposure** effect. Familiarity tends to breed liking (Zajonc, 1968). Proximity may also affect the number of people with whom you are actually likely to meet and interact. The sheer number of peers with whom children come into contact is an important factor affecting the number of friends they are likely to have. Over and above these effects of the community environment on the opportunities for social interaction is its impact on the actual patterns or quality of interactions. To look more specifically at some of these factors I will examine some of the interesting research that has been conducted on the impact of children's home neighbourhoods on their patterns of friendship.

The neighbourhood

The geographic characteristics of children's home neighbourhoods are important factors in their relationships. They may determine if children are able to meet and the form such meetings may take (Medrich *et al.*, 1982). In terms of the direct impact of children's home neighbourhoods on their patterns of interaction, their role in determining the **functional proximity** of children may be more important than simple physical distance. So, for example, accessibility may be more significant than the simple distance between the homes of two children. A neighbourhood with many other children may promote play in large groups and activities which are dependent on such numbers, such as team sports. In comparison, children from neighbourhoods with a low social density, or where there is distance or barriers and obstacles between houses, may have considerably more difficulties in establishing and maintaining friendships (DuBois and Hirsch, 1993). Children who live in houses on the opposite side of a main road or a motorway may find it a considerable obstacle to a relationship. Safety considerations may be an important factor limiting how far afield parents allow their children to play and the types of play and games that are possible. In particularly adverse conditions, meeting friends may need a special effort, possibly even requiring permission or help from parents. Little surprise then that children in these restrictive neighbourhoods tend to have fewer and more formal relationships.

Even if safety and accessibility are not issues, the nature of the local terrain may have a marked impact on children's patterns of play and social interaction. It can limit the space and facilities available to the child. A difficult, hilly terrain may make the playing of many children's games difficult. Just imagine playing football on a steep hill! Similarly, busy roads may cut children off from parks and other areas where numbers of other children may gather and play in relatively large, open spaces. As children get older, the effects of these environmental restrictions on their social activities and their ability to establish and maintain peer relationships may be felt increasingly strongly (Van Vliet, 1981). By adolescence many may come to feel almost as if they are prisoners in their own neighbourhood. The enforced separation from friends may be an especially painful experience for adolescent females because they invest so much intimacy in relationships with only one or a few individuals. Exceptional effort may be required to maintain these relationships under particularly adverse conditions. Fortunately, in modern times the telephone has come to the rescue, to an extent. The use of the telephone by teenage girls will often considerably exceed that required for the simple communication of information; it has become a common means by which adolescent girls seek to establish and maintain their solidarity with friends (Cotterell, 1996).

Toys and equipment

In this section I will examine the role toys and play equipment serve in young children's peer relationships. In particular I will examine the extent to which toys and patterns of the use of play equipment facilitate the initiation of interaction, the way they affect patterns of play, and how children select toys to support their preferred styles of play.

Early theorists argued that young children's peer interaction attempts were to a substantial extent built on and grew out of their interactions with objects, including toys. However, some research with young infants has cast doubts on this view. For example, Vandell *et al.* (1980) showed that there were more frequent and longer sequences of interactions between 6- to 12- month-old infants and their peers in the absence of toys than in the presence of toys. To place this finding in context, the inter- actions of these infants are likely to be fairly brief and often end with at least one of the children showing signs of distress. With the provision of toys, any interaction that does occur may be as the children play independently but are influenced by each other. Although playing independently, they may exchange glances from time to time and sometimes even watch each other or share and exchange toys. This is a much more harmonious and easily managed style of interaction for young children. For young infants, toys are a useful adjunct to social interaction with peers.

The social interaction of toddlers may rely much more directly on their mutual orientation to toys and play materials than is the case with younger infants. From about 12 to 18 months of age, parallel play becomes a prominent feature of children's peer interactions. This is the situation in which children may play with toys near and in parallel with other children but independent of them. This play may occasionally show the beginnings of co-operation, and this increases substantially throughout the succeeding years of childhood as genuine peer relationships begin to emerge and develop (Jacobson, 1981). Some time after it is first apparent, parallel play may serve an important bridging function in children's initiations of social interaction, allowing children to gradually move from playing alone to joining in with another (Bakeman and Brownlee, 1980).

Sex differences in play

Boys and girls typically differ in their preferred toys, play activities and venues (Etaugh and Liss, 1992). Boys are more likely to be involved in active pursuits and team games requiring relatively large amounts of space. Consequently, they are likely to spend much of their time playing outside. Girls, playing in pairs or small groups, often prefer to play indoors, possibly using toys which are typically located there or structures such as the 'home corner' of a primary school classroom. The play of girls is often more highly structured by teacher feedback and adult models. Reflecting these preferences, fantasy play tends to be greater for boys when outdoors and girls when indoors (Sanders and Harper, 1976).

As well as children choosing locations and equipment that support their preferred styles of play, the available equipment and facilities may actually determine patterns of behaviour and levels of conflict (Obanawa and Joh, 1995). Some toys and games, such as cards, may encourage children to play together; others, such as crayons, may encourage solitary play. Toys may also be designed to be played with in specific ways. A bobo doll is meant to be knocked down so that it can roll back up. It has few other uses. In general, highly structured activities encourage compliance and bids for recognition while activities with a low degree of structure produce more displays of initiative, leadership and aggression. Young boys typically favour the low-structure activities, such as playing with blocks or rough and tumble play, and consequently often display more conflict and aggression in their exchanges. In contrast, young girls often prefer more highly structured activities, such as art and playing house, and display correspondingly higher levels of social interaction and co-operation. These differences are to quite a large extent a function of the activity, *not* the sex of the child. When children are observed in activities more typically preferred by the opposite sex, their levels of social interaction and conflict reflect that typically observed in that task context (Carpenter and Huston-Stein, 1980). Sex differences in play may in large part be a reflection of the activities in which children are involved, though there are, of course, sex differences in the preferred play activities of boys and girls. These patterns of preference and use of toys represent an important example of children as active agents in their own socialisation, though the expectations and demands of adults are also a significant influence on children's patterns of free play, toy and equipment use and interaction in general.

Physical environment of the classroom

The physical environment of preschool or school buildings, playgrounds and classrooms has communicative value for its inhabitants. The importance of the school environment for the education process has long been recognised by teachers, who often show great pride in such things as their displays, though its significance often seems to be underestimated by educational planners. The expectations that are conveyed by the school environment may at least in part determine the patterns of behaviour, interactions and relationships of children using the facilities (Ray *et al.*, 1995). Whilst the fixed spaces of the institution (doors, windows, room sizes) are relatively difficult to change, the semi-fixed items (such as furniture) can be easily changed and manipulated to produce corresponding changes in the expectations that are communicated to children and affect their behaviour. For example, seating pupils in small groups around a circle of desks rather than in the more traditional rows and columns of desks can completely change the social climate of a classroom and make it more co-operative and relationship-friendly (Hallinan, 1976).

Most classrooms are, of course, adult designed and may be far from ideal from the child's point of view. But how would children prefer their classroom to be organised? In an interesting study to examine this question, Pfluger and Zola (1974) removed all of the furniture from a nursery school classroom but allowed children to return it and position it as they wished and when they wished. The classroom took on a very different appearance! Large items of furniture, such as the piano and chairs, were not returned to the classroom at all, and most items that did make it back into the room were arranged against the walls, leaving a large, open play area.

Social organisation of the classroom

Given the significance of the education system for Western society it is little surprise that its organisation and structure have been the subject of considerable attention. Often the most effective organisation for instructional purposes is contrasted with that which is most preferred in terms of its impact on children's social relationships. In reality this dichotomy is artificial. Social satisfaction and academic performance are not an either–or dichotomy but rather go hand in hand (Wentzel and Asher, 1995). A positive social climate is conducive to high academic performance and a negative social climate is likely to inhibit academic achievement. Despite the significance and impact of the social organisation of the classroom, relatively little attention is given to the school as a place for the learning of social and relationship skills. A rigid, formal classroom structure can impose such severe restrictions on children's patterns of play and interactions that to all intents and purposes they become institutionalised, devoid of creativity and spontaneity. With the current emphasis on schools as places for learning the three Rs, there is a grave risk that they become impoverished environments for what has been termed the fourth R – relationships (Mand, 1974).

Traditionally, many schools, and adults more generally, have sought to segregate children according to age, sex and ability. Such institutional groupings may make school administration and teaching easier but they may also foster a climate of elitism, inter-group antagonism and discrimination. As an alternative, many other schools have sought to devise organisational structures which avoid these consequences and instead foster a positive, co-operative and generally pro-social climate. To this end, a major contribution has been the use of open classroom formats.

The major difference between traditional and open class-room formats is the degree of personal control that children have over their activities. In a traditional or closed classroom format the teacher is quite directive and the child's activities are fairly closely determined by the teacher. This discourages exploration and is task-oriented. For young children, activities may involve copying tasks or puzzles. Older children may be involved in independent work. These activities necessitate relatively little mobility or social interaction. In contrast, the open classroom uses teaching strategies based on a less structured organisation, encour-ages exploration and emphasises problem-solving and working in small groups. The classroom is acknowledged as a social unit (Neckerman, 1996). In the open classroom young children may be encouraged to play co-operatively with blocks or dolls. Older children may work co-operatively on a problem or undertake a collaborative project within the classroom group. Of course, the choice of an open or closed classroom format is not really this simple and straightforward, and there are certainly many things which can go wrong in trying to implement a flexible, open struc-ture. For example, in the open classroom format, it is important to arrange the work and tasks to ensure that the groups do in practice function co-operatively and involve all their members. If this is not achieved, the greater social freedom for all may actually result in more children becoming socially isolated and neglected as shy, less skilful and assertive individuals are over-looked (Hallinan, 1979). A variety of strategies may be used to ensure the active involvement of all group members. For example, the group may be set problems which are only soluble with input from all of the members, each of whom may have been provided with an essential piece of information. The greater degree of social contact in the well-run open classroom provides more opportunities for friendships to form because of the greater functional proximity of partners; it also tends to produce a more integrated peer friendship network with fewer unreciprocated assertions of friendship (Hallinan, 1976). The open classroom approach allows pupils to appreciate their mutual connectedness, dependence and the potential benefits of co-operative work and interpersonal strategies (Dlugokinski, 1984). Teachers and peers may be perceived as being friendly, supportive and generally more positive than in more formal classroom structures (Johnson and Johnson, 1983). The open style of classroom organisation can produce a much more accepting attitude to peers and school generally (Zahn et al., 1986).

At several points in the earlier chapters of this book I have commented on the commonly observed pattern of sex segregation that characterises children's friendships and play. A study by Bianchi and Bakeman (1978) examined the extent to which this was affected by school organisation. This study compared children in open nursery schools with those in traditional nursery schools which emphasised the active socialisation of the child and conventional standards of behaviour. Although children in both types of school typically spent over 80 per cent of their time in free play with other children, in the traditional school play partners were considerably more likely to be of the same sex. Although parents probably choose nursery schools for their children which reflect their own social values, and hence the effect of the school on relationships may also be caused by this family background factor, this study does nonetheless suggest that we do need to pay attention to the school as a factor in the child's sex-role socialisation.

Social dynamics of the open classroom

The overwhelming weight of evidence seems to show that organisation of a classroom can have very definite effects on children's peer relationships. This raises the question as to the mechanism by which these effects are brought about. This question was addressed by Hallinan and Tuma (1978) in a longitudinal study of children aged approximately 10 to 12 years of age. These authors argued that teaching techniques and the way children are grouped within a classroom affect their proximity and similarity and these in turn affect their relationships. I have already argued that functional proximity is an important factor in children's friendships and that open classroom structures create functional proximity. Similarity is also a well-established factor in children's and adolescents' relationships, and the school has many opportunities to create similarities and differences between children when it assigns them to specific classes to study a set curriculum according to a fixed timetable. Confirming their expectations, these researchers found that children having the same reading teacher and spending more time in a small-group classroom format showed a greater likelihood of choosing each other as friends. As one might expect, the impact of classroom variables was greater on relatively new and weaker relationships rather than strong friendships. Presumably strong, well-established relationships are highly rewarding in themselves and are thus less dependent on environmental contingencies.

The main concern for most parents is that their child's schooling provides them with a sound academic experience. Often, relatively little attention is given to the institution as a place to establish social relationships. And yet schools do take up a considerable part of most children's waking hours and are a place where they meet a great many peers and where many of a child's peer relationships are acted out. Social and academic considerations are not exclusive factors. Quite the contrary, as I have been arguing, they are closely interdependent. Pupils' attitudes to school and academic work are affected by their peer group relationships, which in turn affect the whole social climate and atmosphere of the class. Peer groups are important in everyday classroom functioning. At the extreme, a poor social climate at school can often be the cause of the phenomenon generically labelled 'school phobia'. In contrast, a positive social climate in the school can promote the rapid settling-in of new pupils and improved levels of satisfaction and academic achievement in established pupils (Ladd, 1990). The school as a social institution is certainly a topic worthy of considerable attention.

Summary

In this chapter I have examined the social and cultural context in which children's relationships are played out. In terms of culture, the economic base of a society may determine the structure of social groupings and patterns of family life. At the very simplest level this may determine the number, age and sex of other children that a child encounters. This has considerable implications for the possibility and form of peer relationships. Turning to the role of the family, I first noted that the impact of parents may be greater for younger rather than older children. In terms of family background, I focused mainly on the role of social class and poverty on children's peer relationships. Poverty and family crowding may provide opportunities for social interaction but under such disadvantageous conditions that these may become dysfunctional. Social class may be an important factor in relationships because of differences in socialisation practices. Children from different social classes come to have very different expectations of relationships and views on how they should be managed.

I then moved on to a consideration of how the physical environment may affect relationships. A great deal of children's time with peers is spent either out and about in the home neighbourhood or in the school classroom. Both were discussed to show how they may facilitate or inhibit children's relationship opportunities. Finally, I discussed the impact of school and classroom organisation on children's social networks and friendships. Although school occupies a major part of children's waking hours it is relatively under-valued as a social institution. I discussed the differences between open and traditional classroom formats, and the value of a group problem-solving approach to education. With no loss of academic standards, schools may become a training ground for the fourth R, relationships, as well as other more traditional subjects.

Further reading

Parke, R. D. and Ladd, G. W. (eds) (1992). *Family–peer relationships*. Hillsdale, NJ: Erlbaum. (See Chapter 2 of this volume.)

Schneider, B. H. (1993). *Children's social competence in context*. Toronto: Pergamon. An excellent book that examines in detail the main themes covered in this chapter: the role of the family, school and culture on children's social development and social abilities. A very readable account of relevant theory and research.

Relationship problems

T HE EARLY CHAPTERS OF THIS BOOK examined the basic but changing characteristics of children's friendships over childhood and adolescence. In the preceding chapter these basic patterns were placed in a broader social context. This and the following chapter will try to complete the overall picture by considering relationship problems.

From the earliest days of research into children's relationships there has been a considerable interest in relationship problems. To fully understand healthy relationships it is necessary to understand less well-adapted relationships and their potential implications for later functioning. Only when we understand the nature and implications of relationships in their full diversity can the necessity and form of therapeutic interventions be considered. Before we go any further perhaps a cautionary word is in order. In discussing relationship problems we must be careful not to pigeonhole certain types of relationship as good and other types as bad and needing to be changed. Although there are broad patterns that characterise adaptive relationships, it is all too easy to overlook the fact that there are also substantial individual differences. Relationships are diverse in their form and the crucial question is the extent to which they are adaptive and fulfilling for the participants. Some children prefer just one or two close friendships, others prefer a much broader network. Neither pattern of relating is implicitly better or worse. Each must be judged in terms of the extent to which they fulfil the child's needs.

The above discussion highlights the difficulty of specifying precisely what constitutes a relationship problem. There is no agreed taxonomy of relationship problems (Gottman, 1991). At the simplest, logical level of analysis, relationship difficulties may have their origins in the characteristics of the participants, the situation in which the relationship is played out, or the dynamics of the relationship itself (Doll, 1996). By default, many of these factors have already been touched on in the previous chapters, when examining the factors influencing the formation and growth of relationships. To complicate matters further, many factors associated with relationship difficulties may be both causes and effects, and inextricably linked to a variety of other social, biological and psychological factors. As an example of the difficulty of differentiating problems of cause and effect, social adjustment difficulties may make the establishment of satisfying relationships problematic, but relationship problems may also predispose the child to further social adjustment difficulties.

In this chapter I cover three main themes associated with relationship problems. My first theme focuses on some of the characteristics of individuals that may lead to relationship difficulties. In particular, I examine the impact of physical disabilities, shyness and loneliness on the ability of children to establish and maintain friendships. My second major theme focuses on some of the specific problems of relating that children may encounter. A variety of factors may cause relationships to encounter problems. Some relationship difficulties may quite simply be the result of incompatibilities which are brought out as a relationship develops; other difficulties may be caused by external factors that precipitate a relationship crisis. The third and final theme of the chapter is concerned with the consequences of relationship problems and collapse. Whatever the causes of a relationship collapse, it is likely to entail unpleasant consequences for the individuals concerned. I consider some of the immediate emotional effects of relationship collapse and some of the potentially more serious long-term consequences of dysfunctional patterns of relating.

Physical handicap and disfigurement

The relationships of physically handicapped and disfigured children clearly demonstrate the importance of physical appearance for personal relationships. Children with physical disabilities are perceived as less attractive and are less likely to be chosen as friends (Kleck and De Jong, 1983). These individuals are often deeply aware that others hold negative attitudes towards them and may experience **prejudice** and **discrimination** in many aspects of their life. Perhaps because of their lower popularity and hence fewer opportunities to practise social skills, many physically disabled children also have a poorer knowledge of the strategies for making friends. Ultimately, their own behaviour may come to reflect and anticipate the stereotypic expectations of others.

Visibility is a crucial factor in the stigmatising of a handicap. The more visible a handicap, the more likely it is to disrupt the smooth flow of interaction. Despite their lesser functional implications, problems of appearance may be more stigmatising than a physical disability (Richardson *et al.*, 1961). Facial disfigurements may be especially distracting and disruptive of communication and social interaction as the face is generally visible and an important source of non-verbal information during social interaction (Cash, 1995). For example, vitiligo, a disfiguring skin disorder involving patchy depigmentation of the skin, involves no functional disability but is often a traumatic and socially isolating condition for the sufferer. Perhaps people are unsure about how they are supposed to react and are concerned that normal gaze will be interpreted as staring?

The implication of physical handicap and disfigurement for the individual depends on a number of factors, including the type of disability, age, gender and a variety of situational influences. Even in babies and young infants, prematurity and physical abnormalities may affect the child's attractiveness such that the expectations and behaviour of parents and others are adversely affected (Langlois *et al.*, 1995). Indeed, the attractiveness of young children has even been noted as a potential factor in child abuse (Roscoe *et al.*, 1985).

Because of their relatively limited cognitive abilities, young children tend to categorise others on the basis of their overt physical and behavioural characteristics rather than more abstract personality traits. These categorisations tend to be simple, superficial and exclusive and are the basis for an early and primitive form of prejudice against anyone physically deviant or different. Throughout the nursery-school and primary-school years children show a general preference for non-disabled peers of the same race and sex as themselves. The early secondary-school years may prove even more traumatic for disabled children. This is a time of many changes, the child is settling into a new school, peer relationships are assuming increasing importance and there is a great concern over physical appearance and attractiveness. These factors can result in a great deal of distress for the disfigured adolescent, though other interests and abilities may provide support for their self-esteem and emotional well-being.

Not only is physical appearance associated with social adjustment and achievement, it also affects any remedial treatment which is recommended. In school, teachers are more likely to recommend unattractive children for special class placements (Ross and Salvia, 1975). School psychologists are more likely to recommend less attractive children for places in special mental retardation classes and expect them to experience greater difficulties in peer relationships and future psychological evaluations (Elovitz and Salvia, 1982). These unrealised institutional prejudices are an important cause for concern in our treatment of individuals already battling against widespread prejudice and discrimination.

Shyness

A basic level of shyness may be normal and adaptive in relationships in that it allows social situations to be evaluated before there is a commitment to action. Most of us will experience shyness at some time in our lives. Excessive shyness is a common problem of childhood. Studies of preschoolers have reported 16–30 per cent of children as showing varying degrees of shyness, and this figure generally increases with age up to a peak in early adolescence. More than half of young teenagers report themselves as shy, though then this declines to around the 40 per cent level in adults (Zimbardo, 1977).

The consequences of shyness are as broad as the range of experiences of the condition. The shy child is both attracted to and yet wary of an interaction partner. Shy children take fewer risks with their relationships, often seeking to minimise the likelihood of disapproval rather than trying to gain approval. A shy child may hover on the periphery of a group rather than risk the rejection of a direct attempt at entry (Gottman, 1977). The interactional strategies of shy children result in them generally having fewer and less fulfilling personal relationships (Zimbardo and Radl, 1981), lower self-esteem (Crozier, 1995), higher levels of loneliness (Rubin and Mills, 1988) and, in severe cases, social withdrawal and isolation (Richmond, 1984).

A number of different types of shyness have been distinguished by various authors. At the simplest level we can distinguish between trait and state shyness, also referred to as dispositional and situational shyness (Asendorpf, 1986). Dispositional shyness is shyness as a personality trait, relatively stable and evident in a wide variety of situations. In contrast, situational shyness is the relatively transient result of a specific social situation, especially one that is novel and likely to evoke the attention of others. Of course, in reality most shyness is the product of an interplay between the individual's characteristics and the social situation. For example, schoolchildren often feel shy with strangers but may be considerably less so at home.

Different types of shyness have also been distinguished on the basis of their developmental origins. These have been termed fearful and self-conscious or early and late appearing shyness (Buss, 1986). A strong genetic component has been postulated for fearful shyness and hence it is seen as a relatively enduring individual trait. The stranger-anxiety often regarded as a defining feature of early attachment has been seen as an early example of fearful shyness; it may be seen as the direct precursor of children's shy reactions to strangers throughout the succeeding preschool years (Greenberg and Marvin, 1982). Self-conscious shyness is directly linked to the development of social perspective-taking and children's awareness of themselves as social objects (Buss, 1986). Throughout the preschool years, as children become increasingly aware of themselves as social objects, they realise that they must control their disclosure of thoughts and feelings to others (Rotenberg, 1995). Some children are more aware of their impact on others and this may make them more prone to shyness as they worry about criticism, breaches of privacy, or being different. Mirroring social, physical and cognitive changes, self-consciousness and shyness appear to peak in early adolescence (Zimbardo, 1977).

It is appropriate to conclude this discussion by once again emphasising that situational and personal factors are inextricably linked as causes of shyness. At all ages novelty is a major trigger, though why this is so may change with age. Young children may be shy of new people and situations simply because they do not have the skills to manage the interaction. For older individuals there may be considerably more self-consciousness and emotional baggage involved in shyness.

Loneliness

Loneliness is a negative affective state based on children's perceptions of deficiencies in their social relationships (Peplau and Perlman, 1982). It is closely related to shyness and social rejection (Asher and Wheeler, 1985). Loneliness may take the form of an emotional void resulting from the perceived lack of a close relationship – especially important in the peer relationships of adolescence and beyond – or feelings of marginality and boredom resulting from a perceived inadequacy in the social network (Archibald *et al.*, 1995). Note the word *perceived* in the previous sentence. In reality, the relationships of many lonely children do not markedly differ in number or quality from those of their less lonely counterparts. Indeed, a situationally induced loneliness is a normal part of growing up that is experienced by virtually all children, such as when they change school or the family moves house and the current group of friends is left behind. Fortunately, this experience of loneliness is usually a transient condition.

Although some authors have argued that true loneliness cannot be experienced until the advent of the close peer relationships and abstract modes of thinking of adolescence are developed, few parents or people who work with children would

109

deny that even children as young as 3 can experience the pain of social isolation. Indeed, many researchers looking at attachment across the lifespan emphasise that the working models of relationships that are established in infancy are a foundation and determinant of children's perceptions and evaluations of the status of their later relationships (Shaver and Hazan, 1989). True, loneliness in young children may differ in some of its fine detail from the experience of loneliness of older children and adults, but this does not devalue or deny the developmental continuity of the experience. Children do have well-developed ideas about loneliness and it is still a painful and unpleasant experience to them (Asher and Parker, 1989). From about 9 to 12 years of age, approximately 10 per cent of children report feelings of loneliness (Asher et al., 1984). With the advent of adolescence, peer relationships begin to overtake relationships with parents as sources of support and intimacy and perceived deficiencies in the social network assume a new importance. Loneliness is one of the most frequently mentioned problems of adolescence (Shultz and Moore, 1989).

Loneliness has a variety of psychological and behavioural features, some of which may be both causes and consequences of the condition. Cognitively, the lonely individual may have low self-esteem, a tendency to make self-blaming attributions and generally lower expectations for the outcomes of social interactions. These characteristics are closely related to social skills deficits such as excessive self-attention and inappropriate levels of attention to communication partners. In turn these may lead to inappropriate patterns of self-disclosure and a tendency to make negative judgements of oneself and others, both of which inhibit the establishment of an appropriate level of intimacy with others.

Although much loneliness is situational and relatively transient, for some individuals the cognitive and behavioural features of loneliness may form a vicious circle such that it can become a significantly self-perpetuating condition even into adolescence and adulthood (Hymel and Franke, 1985). For these individuals the problem of how to break the cycle becomes a major issue with substantial implications for later happiness and social adjustment.

Problems of relating

In this section I will focus on the situational and interpersonal characteristics of relationships that may contribute to their decline and dissolution. Perhaps the most important point to stress straight away is that the experience of relationship collapse is an inevitable and normal, perhaps even necessary, part of social development. Learning how to cope with losing and changing friends is complementary to the process of learning how to make and keep friends. That the experience of relationship collapse is a natural part of growing up is illustrated by the age-related patterns of stability in children's friendships. Young children's friendships are less stable than those of older children, at least in part reflecting their less sophisticated cognitive abilities and social skills, especially the skills of conflict management (Hartup *et al.*, 1988). Despite the many vicissitudes of their relationships, young children form friendships relatively easily and in the long run they gain more relationships than they lose. In contrast, the more stable relationships of older children are more intimate and represent a much greater investment. They are considerably more difficult to replace – older children lose more friends than they gain – and their loss is correspondingly more significant for the individuals concerned (Buhrmester and Furman, 1987).

Children's descriptions of broken friendships are considerably less detailed than their accounts of friendship formation though, as with descriptions of friendship, these do increase in complexity as children become more cognitively sophisticated (Bigelow, 1982). At least a part of the explanation for this may be that there are quite simply fewer opportunities for children to refine their account of friendship collapse. Relationships can be dissolved quicker than they can be built, and the process of dissolution may involve a deliberate avoidance of contact and hence a reduction in the opportunities to gather information and refine explanations.

Children often report that some relationships simply drifted apart, as the participants' interests and abilities changed (McCall, 1982). Other relationships are disrupted by external events or major disagreements. A common cause of difficulties lies in the real or perceived violation of the implicit rules of conduct of the relationship (Bigelow *et al.*, 1992). These rules are closely related to children's friendship expectations and change developmentally. In middle-childhood children are less adept at managing conflict than their older counterparts and this is a common cause of relationship disruption. Across all ages, incidents which embarrass or show the partner in a bad light are common explanations for relationship collapse. With the greater intimacy of adolescent relationships, the violation of more abstract rules and expectations becomes an important factor in relationship collapse. Violations of loyalty and trust, exclusivity, and specific standards or patterns of behaviour underlie a substantial majority of the reported explanations of relationship difficulties at this age (Bigelow and La Gaipa, 1980).

Precipitating factors

Despite their undoubted significance, scant attention has been paid to the external events that may precipitate relationship problems for children, for example, moving house or changing school. These sorts of events may be considerably more disruptive for younger and less socially skilled children than for older children or adults as they are likely to have relatively less say or control over the changes that are occurring and may find it more difficult to overcome the obstacles to maintaining current relationships (Venberg *et al.*, 1994). Many children's friendships do not survive these major transitions and their attempts to maintain current relationships are merely providing a buffer against feelings of loneliness and resentment while new friendships are formed.

The move from primary school to secondary school is probably the most common social dislocation experienced by children. Although many children will welcome the move as presenting new challenges, opportunities and a gain in status, it is also a time of anxiety and adjustment (Ladd and Kochenderfer, 1996). Although the transition to secondary school may be made easier for many children by the social support of friends making the same move, the transition is nonetheless likely to be the beginning of a time of great change in friendship networks.

When a family moves house this can be a considerably more challenging and painful prospect for children. Not only will this often entail a change of school, but this is likely to be without the social support of peers undergoing the same experience or a peer social network in the new home neighbourhood. Though most children will quickly settle into their new situation and show few long-term effects, repeated moves can prevent children from establishing and learning about long-term close relationships and this can prove a social handicap in their relationships later in life.

The major problem that children encounter when their family moves house is often the difficulty of gaining entry to already established peer groups. This problem may be most severe for older children, as relatively stable and exclusive cliques may exist. Skill and tenacity may be important if newcomers are to gain acceptance, and even children regarded as skilled and popular in their previous well-established peer groups may have difficulties in establishing new relationships with strangers. In this time of transition, sensitive, supportive family relationships may be crucial to the speed and success of children's adjustment to their new situation. Unfortunately, moving house can also place a stress on family relationships and thus prove doubly disruptive to the child.

Emotional consequences

The emotional impact on the child of the ending of a friendship is often considerably under-estimated by parents and other adults. The precise consequences of the collapse of a relationship are likely to be affected by a number of factors, including the age of the child, their interpretation of the causes of the relationship's collapse, and whether they were the one ending the relationship or the one being dropped.

The collapse of a friendship can be a traumatic experience for children of almost any age, though the significance and nature of the experience may be closely tied to the child's level of relationship understanding. When a friendship collapses the participants will naturally try to understand the causes of the event. For young children with limited cognitive skills, much of the pain of relationship collapse may come from the confusion of not understanding why a supposed friend has terminated a relationship. For older children and adolescents, the pain of relationship collapse may be substantially greater than for their younger counterparts. There are at least two factors underlying this. First, peer relationships become increasingly central to the lives of children as they grow older. By adolescence they are even overtaking relationships with parents as sources of support and nurturance; they are assuming such major significance that even the thought of losing them can produce feelings of jealousy and insecurity. The committed nature of relationships at this age means that a lost relationship would be very difficult to replace. Most of the potential field of eligibles would already be engaged in relatively permanent and exclusive relationships. Second, although the better social cognitive abilities and levels of relationship understanding of older children and adolescents make the collapse of a relationship potentially more comprehensible, this does not necessarily make it a less traumatic event. Quite the contrary, it can make it all the more distressing. Adolescents can give considerable brooding attention to what went wrong with a collapsed relationship (Harvey *et al.*, 1982). Improvements in understanding often lead these older children and adolescents to ponder whether their own characteristics and attributes somehow caused the breakdown. Given the increasing importance of trust and loyalty in older children's friendships, this situation may be especially marked if the child believes that he or she was dropped by the friend who preferred some other peer. This may produce damage to the child's self-esteem, self-blame and personal attributions of incompetence which can be carried forward to affect subsequent patterns of relating. For the sensitive adolescent, even being the one to end a relationship can be difficult because of the recognition of the emotional and social consequences this may have for the other person. Dysfunctional cognitive responses to the collapse of a relationship may produce more disruptive behaviour, social withdrawal, or simply the continued inflexible use of patterns of behaviour that have already proved themselves ineffective (Goetz and Dweck, 1980).

Long-term effects

Many theories of psychotherapy have no hesitation in extolling the significance of early relationships for later social and psychological adjustment. A number of empirical studies have also addressed these issues, though their findings are somewhat less clearcut. A superficial examination of the existing literature does indeed reveal a large number of studies apparently demonstrating that satisfactory early peer relationships are important for later adjustment across a wide range of areas, including the capacity for intimacy in adult relationships, school achievement and dropout rates, anti-social and delinquent behaviour, suicide, criminality and psychological problems and disorders such as alcoholism and even psychosis (Vargo, 1995).

However, the volume of evidence is not everything. Many of the studies in this area are correlational, and the fact that a number of children who experience relationship difficulties early in life grow up to have problems in later life does not prove that the former caused the latter. This evidence could equally well be accounted for in terms of a number of alternative explanations. Perhaps it is the early form of a psychological disorder that will be diagnosed later that is causing the childhood relationship problems rather than the relationship problems causing the later disorder (Parker and Asher, 1987)? Or perhaps a third factor caused both events? Undeniably, many children with relationship problems manage to grow up to be perfectly well adjusted; and many children with good early relationships nonetheless show maladjustment in later life. To cloud matters even further, the methodology of many of the studies contributing to the evidence mentioned above has, unfortunately, been very variable. For example, many have studied unrepresentative groups such as clinic populations, used retrospective accounts of involved parties, anecdotal evidence, or multiple sources whose comparability is unclear. These factors must consequently reduce the confidence one can place in the evidence. Given these difficulties, one can understand why some authors have argued that patterns of influence have been largely assumed rather than proven (Kupersmidt *et al.*, 1990). A useful conclusion to our examination of this debate comes from a review by Parker and Asher (1987). These authors examined the body of evidence for a causal link between childhood relationships and later problems of adjustment and concluded that the strongest associations were between early aggressiveness and later juvenile or adult criminality, and low acceptance in primary school and rates of secondary school drop out. The evidence was weakest in relation to adult psychological disorders. Overall, although it may be difficult to justify all the wide array of claims made for the impact of early relationships on later adjustment, these relationships do nonetheless appear to have a significant effect in several important areas. The magnitude of these effects is such that in severe cases they may certainly justify therapeutic interventions. In less severe cases, one might nonetheless argue for the potential utility of educational programmes to promote healthy patterns of relating. It is to these topics that Chapter 8 is addressed.

Summary

Relationship difficulties can take a number of forms. Some children may have difficulties initiating relationships, others may experience problems in the day-to-day management or successful development of relationships. In this chapter I examined three broad, interrelated causes of relationship difficulties. These three groups of causes were the personal characteristics of the relators, situational factors, and the dynamics of the relationship itself. In terms of personal characteristics, these may be physical, behavioural or psychological. Physical and mental handicaps, disfigurements, psychological disorders and problems of adjustment are likely to make relationships more difficult to establish and maintain, though they may also impact on relationships because of social prejudices. Individual attention was given to two psychological phenomena associated with relationships that have received substantial research attention – shyness and loneliness. These were highlighted as factors that may be both a cause and consequence of relationship problems. The second broad theme in this chapter concerned the impact of situational factors on relationships. Although this is a very ill-defined area of research it is nonetheless clear that situational factors can both directly disrupt some relationships and in other cases exacerbate the impact of other factors. The final part of this chapter examined how the dynamics of relationships themselves can lead to their collapse. Children's cognitive abilities and interests may change, and their expectations and behaviour in the relationship may change as it develops. The causes for these relationship problems lie not with either individual but with natural developmental dynamics of relationships. I ended my review of children's relationship difficulties by considering their implications for later social and psychological adjustment. Although these are sometimes exaggerated, poor early relationships do have implications for later patterns of social adjustment and do raise the issue of intervention as a strategy to promote positive patterns of relating in children.

Further reading

Asher, S. R. and Coie, J. D. (eds) (1990). *Peer rejection in childhood.* Cambridge: Cambridge University Press. As indicated in this chapter, it is now widely accepted that peer rejection can be a particularly damaging cause of social isolation. In Asher and Coie's book the behavioural, cognitive and familial roots of peer rejection are analysed in considerably more detail than was possible in this chapter. The book also contains a series of chapters on the consequences of rejection and issues in intervention that many readers will find particularly interesting and useful.

Rubin, K. H. and Asendorpf, J. (eds) (1993). *Social withdrawal, inhibition, and shyness in childhood.* Hove: Erlbaum. This chapter included a brief discussion of social withdrawal and shyness: this book goes considerably further! It considers methodological issues, biological, temperamental and family factors, communication skills, and how socially withdrawn children perceive themselves and others. Particularly interesting is Kenneth Rubin's chapter on the Waterloo longitudinal project which examines some of the correlates and consequences of social withdrawal in childhood and adolescence.

Chapter 8

Improving peer relationships

As our understanding of the nature and significance of children's peer relationships for their later social and emotional adjustment has improved over the last twenty years or so there has been a corresponding explosion of interest in possible methods of intervention to help those children experiencing relationship difficulties. There are now numerous sophisticated therapeutic approaches for children with relationship difficulties. In this chapter I will initially examine some of the considerations that might lead to a child being regarded as having relationship problems worthy of therapeutic intervention. The main focus of this chapter will be a description and evaluation of the main therapeutic methods that have been used with children experiencing relationship problems.

What is a relationship problem?

Deciding that a child has relationship problems worthy of intervention can be a considerably more complicated matter than might at first be imagined. One major complication is that different people may elicit different patterns of behaviour from the child and they may evaluate it differently. Teachers, parents and peers may differ quite considerably in what they regard as a problematic pattern of behaviour and consequently in their evaluation of a child. Teachers may regard the quiet, obedient child as well adjusted to school. These traits may not be great recommendations in the eyes of the peer group. It is only fairly gross difficulties that are likely to find substantial levels of agreement. Even if different judges do manage to agree that a child has serious problems, they will often differ in how they think these problems would be best addressed. The conflicting demands and expectations on the child may make it difficult to maintain any gains from therapy.

Perhaps the person who is most knowledgeable about a child's peer relationships is the child him- or herself. Children's self-reports of the status of their relationships correlate well with evaluations derived from other sources and have been highlighted as potentially valuable indicators of their social adjustment and satisfaction with their relationships, though this source of information may be limited by the individual child's cognitive and verbal abilities. Each method of assessment has its advantages and disadvantages. A balanced approach would aim to use several sources of assessment information in order to provide a broad and balanced picture of the child in its multiple contexts (Inderbitzen, 1994).

Matching problems and therapies

Most social skills training programmes operate on the basis of a **deficit model** of social skills. In other words, maladapted children are compared with their better adapted counterparts of the same age and sex and the behavioural or cognitive differences that exist between them are assumed to be possible causes of their differences in social adaptation. Of course, this still leaves it up to the therapist to decide where to look for such differences.

Most studies of social skills training with socially isolated children have sought to define social isolation in one or more of three main ways, and these different indices are not always closely correlated. First, in terms of the amount of time a child spends interacting with peers. Second, in terms of the quality of the child's peer interactions. And third, in terms of the child's peer popularity, often assessed by means of a technique **sociometry**. Each of these approaches to defining social isolation would suggest specific aims or approaches to therapy which are appropriate in certain circumstances but can have considerable shortcomings in others. For example, defining social isolation in terms of the simple and fairly intuitive criterion of the amount of time spent in social interaction would pick up the socially neglected child but might overlook aggressive, actively rejected children. They may be interacting at high levels but in ways aversive to their peers! Although an **intervention** programme aimed simply at increasing levels of interaction could be useful for socially neglected children, it might actually exacerbate the problems of an aggressive child. In contrast, focusing on quality of interaction would certainly pick up the aggressive child, but might miss the neglected child whose interactions are positive but of excessively low frequency. Intervention programmes designed to reduce aggressiveness and teach communication skills and pro-social behaviour might be useful for aggressive, rejected children but less appropriate for the neglected social isolate.

The different ways of defining social isolation have resulted in relatively little agreement over what constitutes a genuine deficit worthy of intervention and, importantly, how we should measure the success of our interventions. Interventions aimed at changing specific behaviours often appear more effective than those trying to improve peer evaluations, but what is the value of a behavioural change if it does not impact on the child's social acceptability to his or her peers? Peer reputation is an important predictor of later adjustment. There are a great many issues to be resolved before we fully understand the uses and limitations of different indices in assessing the need for and success of therapeutic interventions for children with relationship problems.

Social skills training

A variety of cognitive and behavioural skills is necessary for successful social interaction. Skills deficits may be the result of a lack of knowledge of what is appropriate behaviour in a given situation, lack of actual behavioural skills, or an inability to monitor and modify ongoing skilled performance. Cognitive–behavioural interventions in general, and social skills training in particular, may address any or all of these deficits in order to promote successful social interaction (Blonk *et al.*, 1996). The prime assumption of social skills training is that interactional skills, like other behavioural skills, can be taught.

The causes of a child's social isolation, the characteristics of the child (e.g. age, sex, social class and ethnic group), and the characteristics of the child's broader social network may all be important considerations when designing an intervention programme appropriate to a specific child. The intervention strategy adopted is likely to be determined both by the problem identified and the theoretical orientation of a particular therapist. Although relevant, most intervention studies appear to give relatively scant attention to how children's cognitive or communication abilities may impact on the effectiveness of techniques. This is particularly unfortunate as a review by Schneider (1992) does suggest that, for example, techniques such as modelling, which require less cognitive mediation, are most effective with preschoolers and more complex, multi-technique approaches based on **coaching** may be more effective with older, more cognitively sophisticated children.

In the following sections I will examine several approaches to intervention that have received considerable attention in the relationships literature. Shaping and modelling are basic behavioural methods concerned with the learning and modification of behaviour. These can be particularly useful for teaching or promoting fairly specific patterns of behaviour which are either new or low in frequency in the current repertoire of the child. Cognitive approaches give more consideration to the way children think about relationships. The idea here is that if the way a child perceives and thinks about relationships can be changed then the child's pattern of social behaviour should also change correspondingly. Although the behavioural and cognitive approaches are used exclusively by some therapists, they each have their advantages and drawbacks and so are commonly combined in a broad-based programme which also includes direct instruction in relevant social skills.

An increasingly important alternative to traditional social skills training programmes is based on the idea that it is the social context which maintains maladaptive patterns of relating. The failure to take the social context of relationships into account may explain why many social skills interventions fail to demonstrate the generalisation to other situations and maintenance of therapeutic gains much beyond the immediate training period. A supportive peer context has important adaptive functions in its own right but could certainly be usefully combined with other social skills training procedures.

Shaping

Shaping is the use of rewards to boost the frequency of behaviours which increasingly approximate to some desired form. For example, in the classic case study of 'Ann', social rewards such as praise and attention were used to gradually increase a 4-year-old girl's rates of social interaction with peers (Allen *et al.*, 1964). As well as simple rates of social interaction, shaping has also been used to increase levels of prosocial behaviour and decrease levels of aggressive behaviour in young children. Both factors are important in children's peer relationships. Shaping is amongst the most powerful intervention techniques used to help socially isolated children (Schneider, 1992), though it may be difficult to use with extreme isolates who provide very little spontaneous behaviour to be shaped. In these cases, or where very specific or complex skills are required, combining the technique with other procedures, such as coaching or modelling, in a broader social skills training programme often proves effective.

A major issue with shaping concerns the stability and generalisation of therapeutic improvements. Many studies which have shown rapid and substantial short-term gains have failed to maintain these through to a follow-up some weeks or months after the intervention has finished. One reason for the difficulty in maintaining therapeutic gains may be that behavioural programmes tend to be fairly short in duration, though social interaction is supposed to be intrinsically rewarding and hence self-sustaining. A more gradual fading out of the external rewards for the desired behaviour, and teaching the child self-reinforcement and self-monitoring procedures, may help maintain change in the face of disinterest or even negative reactions from others (Meichenbaum, 1986). The specific behavioural changes achieved through shaping may often benefit by being underpinned by changes in the child's social cognitive processes and more fully embedded into the broader set of interrelated skills required to sustain social inter-action. A broader social skills training programme, which also includes elements of social problem-solving, cognitive therapy and modelling, may provide a more substantial foundation for the maintenance of therapeutic change (Albano *et al.*, 1995).

Modelling

Modelling is the learning of new patterns of behaviour through observing another person (the model). It allows the transmission of new skills and may facilitate or inhibit the use of existing skills. This is not just a method of therapy – even young children quite naturally use modelling in their everyday lives. They often copy the behaviour of peers, especially those who are admired or who are achieving some desired reward through the use of the behaviour, and they may even be rewarded by their peers for this imitation.

Modelling may be live or symbolic (on film). This latter approach can confer a significant advantage on modelling as a therapeutic technique – it can be used in fairly brief sessions with quite large groups of children by relatively unskilled personnel. This can make it a valuable addition to other intervention techniques or recommend it for use in skills training programmes in schools, for example.

A number of studies of children from preschool to adolescence have demonstrated the effective use of modelling to improve children's relationship skills (see Erwin, 1993). The appropriateness of the model is an important factor. The use of similar models (e.g. of the same age and sex) who are liked is generally most effective (Schunk, 1987). Modelling is also more effective when the reward value of the modelled behaviours is emphasised, whether this is within the film itself or through a therapist's comments.

The difficulty of implementing complex new patterns of social behaviour suggests that shaping and modelling procedures could be usefully combined. The initial success of a modelling intervention is comparable with that achieved by shaping though, as with shaping, a major issue in the use of the technique concerns the stability of any behavioural improvements. Modelling theory does recognise the role of rewards in the learning and performance of modelled behaviours and the combining of modelling and shaping procedures could increase both the immediate and longer-term effectiveness of an intervention programme for children with peer relationship problems (Perry and Furukawa, 1986).

Social problem solving

The difficulties experienced by many socially isolated children derive not from deficits in their behavioural repertoires but from their inability to identify the behaviours and responses appropriate for certain situations. The social problem solving approach to therapy gives focus to the cognitive abilities that underpin behavioural skills. It aims to promote social adaptation by giving children a better understanding of the causes and consequences of their behaviour. Good social problem solving abilities are associated with a variety of positive interpersonal outcomes, including the ability to make friends easily and having many friends. Social problem solving deficits are associated with negative interpersonal behaviours and aggressiveness in children, characteristics which often lead to active rejection by peers (Marsh et al., 1981). Social problem solving programmes may be most effective with these individuals (Rubin, 1985). For example, training in social role-taking abilities has been shown to reduce levels of negative behaviour and increase levels of positive behaviours in delinquents (Chalmers and Townsend, 1990).

In their Interpersonal Cognitive Problem Solving (ICPS) approach to therapy, Spivack and Shure (1989) identify a number of problem solving skills that are important in relationships, including the ability to identify problems, to focus on the major features rather than peripheral aspects of a problematic situation, to understand the relationship between interpersonal motives and actions, to identify the means to achieve a desired end, to think in terms of alternative solutions to problems, and to anticipate the consequences of actions. Different skills may be important for different individuals and at different ages. For example, means–end thinking is a higher order skill that does not emerge until middle-childhood. An important point to stress here is that ICPS programmes aim to teach a basic set of cognitive skills which children can use to generate and choose between a variety of solutions appropriate to their interpersonal problems; it does not aim to teach children *the* solution to a particular problem.

ICPS programmes have been reported with children from preschool age upwards. A common procedure is for small groups of children to meet for a number of sessions to discuss problem vignettes. A typical vignette, for example, might consist of the situation in which two children each want to play with the same toy. The role of the trainer is to ensure that the whole group is involved in the activity and to facilitate the generation of alternative solutions, or the use of whatever other skill is being trained. Training programmes have shown improvements in children's problem solving abilities, social adjustment, social orientation and peer status (Shure, 1993). A considerable recommendation for preventative ICPS programmes is that improvements are often most marked for those children who are initially the least well socially adapted.

Despite the positive example given above, many ICPS interventions are considerably less successful, and frequently appear to produce improvements in children's problem solving skills without any consequent changes in their behaviour or evaluations by peers (Erwin, 1996). Research reviews have suggested that social problem solving therapies are generally less effective than shaping, modelling or coaching interventions, though this general picture may be excessively pessimistic and biased by the concentration of much ICPS research on preventative programmes (Schneider, 1992). There is less room for improvement in already relatively well-adjusted populations. Despite the doubts that have been cast on cognitive problem solving therapies as a sole method of intervention for children with relationship difficulties, at the very least they may have a useful role in helping the generalisation and stability of improvements brought about by other approaches. For example, they may help children to appreciate the limitations and potential of other forms of training. Children may be helped to see the strategies and behaviours acquired through other techniques as coming from a range of possibilities with probabilistic rather than guaranteed outcomes. This may help to prepare them for the inevitable difficulties and setbacks which occur as training is transferred to real-life situations.

Coaching

Coaching is the teaching of specific new social and cognitive skills through direct instruction and practice. It has been seen by some authors as being more of an educational than a therapeutic technique (Goldstein *et al.*, 1985). Advocates of this approach argue that the maintenance and generalisation of treatment effects is enhanced by promoting the understanding of a skill and an ability to self-monitor and adapt performance. Supporting this, Mize and Ladd (1990) showed that improvements from social skills training correlated with improvements in children's knowledge of social strategies.

In practice, coaching is usually used in conjunction with elements of the behavioural and cognitive approaches outlined in the preceding sections, such as modelling, role play, **cognitive restructuring** and the direct reinforcement of effective behaviours. In this guise it becomes an extremely powerful intervention technique. A typical coaching sequence might consist of three phases. In the first phase, the tuition phase, the child would be given a rule or example of an effective behaviour. For example, the child may be shown a film or perhaps a skilled peer engaging in an activity such as asking to join a group at play. In the second phase, the rehearsal phase, the child would practise the behaviour. This could include elements of role playing. Finally, in the third phase, the review phase, the child is given feedback and suggestions for improvement by the trainer, or other children if the training programme is group-based. With appropriate changes, the cycle may then be repeated, or another problem addressed.

Coaching can be used for children with fairly complex social difficulties. Some children may not appreciate that certain of their behaviour patterns and expectations underlie their poor social status; they may not be aware that there are alternative behavioural strategies open to them; may know but be unable to enact appropriate social behaviours; or may simply be over-anxious about some social situations. The skills taught in a coaching programme can potentially address any or all of these issues and might include things such as initiating interaction, leading (offering useful suggestions and directions), giving and receiving positive interaction, asking questions, and making supportive statements. Coaching techniques have been successfully used with socially rejected children and adolescents (e.g. Murphy and Schneider, 1994). In these days of limited economic resources, coaching programmes also have the major advantage that they are often relatively brief and improvements have demonstrated relatively good levels of stability. In a programme consisting of only 30 minutes per day for one week, Gottman *et al.* (1976) produced marked changes which lasted through to a follow-up nine weeks later. Some social skills training programmes also report the added bonus of improvements in the social behaviour of the untrained acquaintances of the child who was trained (Cooke and Apolloni, 1976)!

There is a substantial literature attesting to the efficacy of coaching procedures with socially neglected children with low levels of popularity. Though somewhat less developed, evidence concerning its effectiveness with disruptive and rejected children and adolescents is also starting to accumulate. Gresham and Nagle (1980) found that coaching was particularly effective at decreasing rates of negative interaction. Portuguese and American research using coaching procedures has shown that it is possible to obtain substantial amounts of voluntary participation and improvement in the behaviour of delinquent adolescents (e.g. Matos *et al.*, 1991).

Peer contact as therapy

For some children with handicaps and disfigurements their social isolation has its roots directly in the stereotypes and values of their peer group. In these circumstances, peer group contact can be important in helping to dispel many of the faulty assumptions and evaluations which underlie a child's social isolation (Richardson *et al.*, 1974). Even in non-handicapped children the peer group may sustain a previously established reputation, and reduce the generalisation and long-term stability of the changes brought about by social skills training. Conversely, directly altering the social structures that originated and maintain the social isolation of a child can prove an extremely effective approach to intervention. In this section I will examine some of the variety of approaches that have aimed to use the child's peer group as an agent of change.

At the simplest level, directly reinforcing and coaching an isolated child's peer group can be used to encourage the children to interact with a withdrawn peer. Pairing children with more socially skilled, popular peers can also promote improvements in the social skills and status of neglected or isolated children (Morris *et al.*, 1995). A subtle approach to reducing friction and encouraging positive relationships within a peer group has been to structure activities to encourage co-operative interactions to achieve specific goals and rewards. These situations then provide the isolated child with opportunities to model, practise and be rewarded for appropriate behaviour and to disconfirm other children's negative attitudes and avoidance behaviours. This approach has the added advantage that it can be fairly readily integrated into the ordinary school classroom and curriculum.

A concrete example will best illustrate how a **co-operative learning** group might operate. If a particular foreign country was to be studied in a geography lesson, the material could be divided amongst the group members such that a child covers a different aspect of the material (social, economic, physical geography, etc.) but all the different fragments are required to gain a complete picture (Aronson, 1991). An important point here is that the group interactions must be carefully managed and structured. Group members must be interdependent and outcomes must be positive or else some group members may be ignored, blamed for failures and further ostracised. In general, co-operative learning programmes are likely to be most effective and improvements best maintained if they are integrated into a standard teaching programme rather than conducted as short-term interventions. Research on the effects of co-operative learning programmes suggests that they may produce a variety of positive social outcomes for socially isolated children, including improvements in self-esteem and feelings of social efficacy, role-taking abilities, evaluations by peers, popularity and levels of social interaction (e.g. Siner, 1993). However, group experience may have relatively little effect on levels of social skills and may not be sustained and generalised to other situations without additional procedures such as coaching (Bierman and Furman, 1984). As one of the potential problems with coaching is the translation of behavioural improvements into long-term improvements in the child's social network, these two techniques may be well-suited companions in an intervention programme.

Cross-age interaction

Many children become socially neglected simply because they cannot hold their own in the free-for-all of social interaction with their age mates – they are responsive but lack the skills to initiate and direct interactions successfully. For these individuals (and many young children) complex interventions based on the use of highly structured activities to manage peer contacts may not be particularly appropriate or necessary. Even relatively limited opportunities to practise social interaction can dramatically improve their social skills. One approach to helping these children has been to give them the experience of successful interaction by partnering them with slightly younger children. For example, in a study by Furman et al. (1979) isolated preschoolers were partnered with children 12 to 20 months younger than themselves for a series of play sessions. Rates of social interaction increased dramatically for the isolated children during the arranged play sessions, and to a large extent these were maintained when the children returned to their normal classrooms. The effectiveness of this programme seemed to lie in the fact that in their play with younger children the older, socially isolated children were learning how to co-operate with and help their less able play partner. These relatively mature, pro-social patterns of relating are major characteristics of the relationships of older children and so this practice seemed to pay important dividends in their relationships with their age mates.

Summary

This chapter examines the use of therapeutic interventions for children with relationship difficulties. An immediate problem one encounters when considering the feasibility of such interventions is the difficulty of actually defining what constitutes a relationship problem. Parents, teachers and the child itself may disagree about what is acceptable and what is a problematic pattern of relating. Taking several views into account may be advisable. Many factors have to be taken into consideration when devising an intervention strategy for use with an isolated child. These are likely to include the child's age, sex, possibly ethnic background, and the type of relationship problem. Some children possess the necessary skills for social interaction but are nonetheless neglected by their peer group. Here the rate of interaction needs to be increased. Other children may be overlooked or even actively rejected because they lack the skills for effective interaction with peers. For these children, an intervention may focus on improving their cognitive and behavioural skills. I outlined several intervention strategies. Shaping is the simple use of rewards to gradually alter patterns of behaviour in some desired direction. Modelling is the use of skilled individuals to provide examples of behaviour which the child may learn and then use in its own interactions. Social problem solving approaches concentrate on improving the way children think about their interactions, to make them more predictable and controllable and hence more likely to deliver the outcomes desired by the child. Coaching is a technique which uses direct instruction, rehearsal and feedback to help children hone their interactional skills. Most social skills programmes tend to

combine elements of several approaches. Many social skills programmes have reported difficulties with the long-term maintenance
and generalisation of therapeutic gains to other social contexts.
Social skills training often gives insufficient recognition to the role
of social context in maintaining patterns of social behaviour and
social status. An alternative to the social skills training approach
to intervention may be to provide children with the opportunity
for positive, co-operative interactions with peers which can serve
as a natural training ground for improving social skills. Social
skills training and peer contact approaches are not necessarily
exclusive and in combination they may provide an extremely
powerful tool for producing effective and relatively permanent
change. The techniques covered in this chapter can and have been
used in schools, and in preventative as well as remedial programmes. It may be in the realm of prevention that their greatest
and as yet largely unrealised potential lies, as part of a school
curriculum which trains social and interpersonal skills as well as
academic abilities.

Further reading

Hansen, D. J., Nangle, D. W. and Ellis, J. T. (1996). Reconsideration of
the use of peer sociometrics for evaluating social skills training.
Behavior Modification, 20, 281–99. As mentioned in this chapter,
sociometry is a common but sometimes controversial technique used
in many studies of social skills training. I recommend this article
as an example of a recent study into the validity of the technique.
It raises questions as to the stability of individual assessments of
sociometric status.

Schneider, B. H. (1992). Didactic methods for enhancing children's peer
relations: a quantitative review. *Clinical Psychology Review*, 12,
363–82. In this chapter a number of different approaches to social
skills training with children were outlined. This article is an important meta-analytic review comparing the effectiveness of these
different types of social skills training with children. Effectiveness is
considered in terms of a variety of outcome criteria, the impact of
moderating variables and the long-term stability of any treatment
gains. This paper may be hard going but it is well worth the effort.

Glossary

The first occurrence of each of these terms is highlighted in **bold** type in the main text.

acquaintanceship The *process* of relationship development.

aggression Physical or verbal behaviour intended to harm another.

attachment The emotional bond between two individuals, most commonly used to refer to the early mother–child relationship. Often classified as secure, avoidant or resistant.

attribution The process of inferring traits and dispositions in others.

authoritarian style of parenting A restrictive, punitive style.

authoritative style of parenting A nurturant style using explanation and negotiation of rules.

coaching A therapeutic approach stressing direct instruction.

cognitive restructuring Changing self-defeating or maladaptive patterns of thinking or beliefs so they become more logical or self-enhancing.

consensual validation   The social as compared with objective affirmation of an individual's attitudes, opinions, values, etc.

co-operative learning   An instructional method which stresses interdependent learning in groups.

deficit model   Defines social skills problems in terms of a lack of the behaviours possessed by more socially successful individuals.

discrimination   Differential behaviour towards an individual because of their personal characteristics (e.g. race, gender, disability).

display rules   Cultural norms about acceptable patterns of expressive behaviour in specific situations.

empathy   The ability to appreciate another's feelings.

friendship   A close reciprocal relationship that has developed over time.

functional proximity   The degree to which the social and physical environment permits contact between individuals.

gender role   The social expectations about how males and females should think and act.

generalisation   The extent to which a therapeutic gain is transferred to new situations.

humanistic psychology   An approach emphasising personal interpretation and experience; individuals are seen as intrinsically good and self-healing.

impression management   Controlling one's behaviour to convey specific impressions.

intervention   A programme of therapy.

isolate   An individual with few or no friends.

loneliness   Aversive state resulting from a mismatch in the individual's perceived and desired social relationships.

mere exposure hypothesis   The idea that familiarity alone can affect our evaluation of objects and people.

modelling   The learning of behaviour from observing its performance by another person (the model).

neglected status   A sociometric classification in which children are isolated but not actively rejected by their peers.

norms   Rules and standards that govern behaviour within a specific group.

peers   Individuals of about the same age or behavioural level.

prejudice   An attitude, usually negative, applied to an individual because of their membership of some group (e.g. racial or gender).

propinquity   Nearness (proximity).

reinforcement   A consequence that increases the probability of a behaviour occurring.

rejected status A sociometric classification reflecting that an individual is actively disliked and avoided.

role play A behavioural rehearsal in which a person practises responses in a social situation or plays the part of some other person; often used in counselling and training exercises.

role-taking The ability to adopt the perspective of another.

rough and tumble play A physical, assertive style of play.

schema A cognitive structure representing an individual's knowledge about an object or situation.

self-actualisation A basic tendency, proposed by humanistic psychologists, in which there is openness to new experience and a genuine realisation and expression of the core self.

self-concept The individual's sense of identity, of who you are.

self-disclosure The voluntary revelation of personal information.

self-esteem The degree to which there is concordance between the actual and ideal self.

shaping A basic method of behavioural therapy in which rewards are used to increase the frequency of behaviours which increasingly approximate some desired form.

shyness Social anxiety inhibiting social interaction.

social class Categorisation of people based on criteria such as income, education and life-style.

social cognitive Relates to social cognition, the cognitive processes underpinning social knowledge and behaviour.

social comparison The motivation to validate one's opinions, attitudes and abilities by comparing them with those held by other people.

social network The interrelated and connected set of people comprising an individual's social contacts.

social referencing The use of cues from others as a guide to appropriate reactions to objects and events.

social skills The repertoire of behaviours appropriate to social interaction.

social skills training A therapeutic approach that believes social behaviour can be trained in much the same way as any other skill.

sociometry A popular method of assessing social preferences and popularity.

stereotyping The cognitive component of prejudice. A faulty and inflexible generalisation applied to an individual because of their membership of some social group (e.g. racial or gender).

Strange Situations Test A common method of assessing attachment classifications.

working model The internalised expectations of relationships.

References

Aboud, F. E. (1988). *Children and prejudice.* Oxford: Blackwell.

Adler, P. A. and Adler, P. (1995). Dynamics of inclusion and exclusion in preadolescent cliques. *Social Psychology Quarterly*, 58, 145–62.

Ainsworth, M. D. S. (1989). Attachment beyond infancy. *American Psychologist*, 44, 709–16.

Ainsworth, M. D. S., Blehar, M. C., Waters, E. and Wall, S. (1978). *Patterns of attachment: a psychological study of the strange situation.* Hillsdale, NJ: Erlbaum.

Albano, A. M., Marten, P. A., Holt, C. S. and Heimberg, R. G. (1995). Cognitive-behavioral group treatment for social phobia in adolescents. *Journal of Nervous and Mental Diseases*, 183, 649–56.

Allen, K. E., Hart, B., Buell, J. S., Harris, F. R.

and Wolf, M. M. (1964). Effects of social reinforcement of isolate behavior on a nursery school child. *Child Development*, 35, 511–18.

Archibald, F. S., Bartholomew, K. and Marx, R. (1995). Loneliness in early adolescence: a test of the cognitive discrepancy model of loneliness. *Personality and Social Psychology Bulletin*, 21, 296–301.

Aronson, E. (1991). *The social animal* (6th edn). New York: Freeman.

Asendorpf, J. (1986). Shyness in middle and late childhood. In: W. H. Jones, J. M. Cheek and S. R. Briggs (eds), *Shyness: perspectives on research and treatment*. New York: Plenum.

Asher, S. R., Hymel, S. and Renshaw, P. D. (1984). Loneliness in children. *Child Development*, 55, 1457–64.

Asher, S. R. and Parker, J. G. (1989). Significance of peer relationship problems in childhood. In: B. H. Schneider, G. Attili, J. Nadel and R. P. Weissberg (eds), *Social competence in developmental perspective*. Dordrecht: Kluwer.

Asher, S. R. and Wheeler, V. A. (1985). Children's loneliness: a comparison of rejected and neglected peer status. *Journal of Consulting and Clinical Psychology*, 53, 500–5.

Azmitia, M. and Montgomery, R. (1993). Friendship, transactive dialogues, and the development of scientific reasoning. *Social Development*, 2, 202–21.

Bakeman, R. and Brownlee, J. R. (1980). The strategic use of parallel play: a sequential analysis. *Child Development*, 51, 873–8.

Balding, J. (1993). *Young people in 1992*. Exeter: University of Exeter.

Barnett, M. A. (1984). Similarity of experience and empathy in preschoolers. *Journal of Genetic Psychology*, 145, 241–50.

Belle, D. (1989). Gender differences in children's social networks and social supports. In: D. Belle (ed.), *Children's social networks and social supports*. New York: Wiley

Belsky, J., Campbell, S. B., Cohn, J. F. and Moore, G. (1996). Instability of infant–parent attachment security. *Developmental Psychology*, 32, 921–4.

Berndt, T. J. and Das, R. (1987). Effects of popularity and friendship on perception of the personality and social behavior of peers. *Journal of Early Adolescence*, 7, 429–39.

Berndt, T. J. and Hoyle, S. G. (1985). Stability and change in childhood and adolescent friendships. *Developmental Psychology*, 21, 1007–15.

Berndt, T. J. and Zook, J. M. (1993). Effects of friendship on adolescent development. *Bulletin of the Hong Kong Psychological Society*, 30–31, 15–34.

Bianchi, B. D. and Bakeman, R. (1978). Sex-typed preferences observed in preschoolers: traditional and open school differences. *Child Development*, 49, 910–12.

Bierman, K. L. and Furman, W. (1984). The effects of social skills training and peer involvement on the social adjustment of preadolescents. *Child Development*, 55, 151–62.

Bigelow, B. J. (1982). Disengagement and development of social concepts. Paper to the International Conference on Personal Relationships, University of Wisconsin at Madison, July.

Bigelow, B. J. and La Gaipa, J. J. (1975). Children's written descriptions of friendship: a multi-dimensional analysis. *Developmental Psychology*, 11, 857–8.

Bigelow, B. J. and La Gaipa, J. J. (1980). The development of friendship values and choice. In: H. C. Foot, A. J. Chapman and J. R. Smith (eds), *Friendship and social relations in children*. Chichester: Wiley.

Bigelow, B. J., Tesson, G. and Lewko, J. H. (1992). The social rules that children use: close friends, other friends, and 'other kids' compared to parents, teachers, and siblings. *International Journal of Behavioral Development*, 15, 315–35.

Blonk, R. W. B., Prins, P. J. M., Sergeant, J. A. and Ringrose, J. (1996). Cognitive-behavioral group therapy for socially incompetent children: short-term and maintenance effects with a clinical sample. *Journal of Clinical Child Psychology*, 25, 215–24.

Boivin, M. and Hymel, S. (1997). Peer experiences and social perceptions. *Developmental Psychology*, 33, 135–45.

Bowlby, J. (1969). *Attachment and loss, vol. 1: Attachment*. London: Hogarth Press.

Braza, F., Braza, P., Carreras, M. R. and Munoz, J. M. (1997). Development of sex differences in preschool children. *Psychological Reports*, 80, 179–88.

Bretherton, I. (1984). Social referencing and the interfacing of minds. *Merrill Palmer Quarterly*, 30, 419–27.

Brookes-Gunn, J. and Paikoff, R. L. (1992). Changes in self-feelings during the transition towards adolescence. In: H. McGurk (ed.), *Childhood social development*. Hove: Erlbaum.

Brown, B. B. (1982). The extent and effects of peer pressure among high school students. *Journal of Youth and Adolescence*, 11, 121–33.

Brown, B. B., Eicher, S. A. and Petrie, S. (1986). The importance of peer group ('crowd') affiliation in adolescence. *Journal of Adolescence*, 9, 73–95.

Brown, J. R., Donelan-McCall, N. and Dunn, J. (1996). Why talk about mental states? The significance of children's conversations with friends, siblings, and mothers. *Child Development*, 67, 836–49.

Buhrmester, D. and Furman, W. (1987). The development of companionship and intimacy. *Child Development*, 58, 1101–13.

Bukowski, W. M., Pizzamiglio, M. T., Newcomb, A. F. and Hoza, B. (1996). Popularity as an affordance for friendship. *Social Development*, 5, 189–202.

Burks, V. S. and Parke, R. D. (1996). Parent and child representations of social relationships. *Merrill Palmer Quarterly*, 42, 358–78.

Burleson, B. R. and Samter, W. (1994). A social skills approach to relationship maintenance. In: D. J. Canary and L. Stafford (eds), *Communication and relational maintenance*. San Diego, CA: Academic Press.

Buss, A. H. (1986). A theory of shyness. In: W. H. Jones, J. M. Cheek and S. R. Briggs (eds), *Shyness: perspectives on research and treatment*. New York: Plenum.

Buss, A. H. and Plomin, R. (1984). *Temperament: early developing personality traits*. San Francisco, CA: Freeman.

Carpenter, C. J. and Huston-Stein, A. (1980). Activity structure and sex-typed behavior in preschool children. *Child Development*, 51, 862–72.

Cash, T. F. (1995). Developmental teasing about physical appearance: retrospective descriptions and relationships with body image. *Social Behavior and Personality*, 23, 123–9.

Chalmers, J. B. and Townsend, M. A. R. (1990). The effects of training in social perspective taking on socially maladjusted girls. *Child Development*, 61, 178–90.

Chess, S., Thomas, A. and Cameron, M. (1976). Sexual attitudes and behavior patterns in a middle-class adolescent population. *American Journal of Orthopsychiatry*, 46, 689–701.

Claes, M. E. (1992). Friendship and personal adjustment during adolescence. *Journal of Adolescence*, 15, 39–55.

Clark, M. L. and Ayers, M. (1992). Friendship similarity during early adolescence. *Journal of Psychology*, 126, 393–405.

Clark, M. L. and Ayers, M. (1993). Friendship expectations and friendship evaluations: reciprocity and gender effects. *Youth and Society*, 24, 299–313.

Coates, D. L. (1987). Gender differences in the structure and support characteristics of Black adolescents' social networks. *Sex Roles*, 17, 667–87.

Cohn, D. A., Patterson, C. J. and Christopoulos, C. (1991). The family and children's peer relations. *Journal of Social and Personal Relationships*, 8, 315–46.

Coleman, J. (1995). Adolescence in a changing world. In: S. Jackson and H. Rodriguez-Tomé (eds), *Adolescence and its social worlds*. Hove: Erlbaum.

Coleman, J. C. and Hendry, L. (1990). *The nature of adolescence*. London: Routledge.

Cooke, T. and Apolloni, T. (1976). Developing positive social emotional behaviors: a study of training and generalization effects. *Journal of Applied Behavioral Analysis*, 9, 65–78.

Cooley, C. H. (1912). *Human nature and the social order*. New York: Scribner.

Corsaro, W. A. (1994). Discussion, debate, and friendship processes: peer discourse in U.S. and Italian nursery schools. *Sociology of Education*, 67, 1–26.

Cotterell, J. (1996). *Social networks and social influences in adolescence*. London: Routledge.

Crozier, W. R. (1995). Shyness and self-esteem in middle childhood. *British Journal of Educational Psychology*, 65, 85–95.

Csikszentmihalyi, M. and Larson, R. (1984). *Being adolescent*. New York: Basic Books.

Csikszentmihalyi, M., Larson, R. and Prescott, S. (1977). The ecology of adolescent activity and experience. *Journal of Youth and Adolescence*, 6, 281–94.

DeKlyen, M. (1996). Disruptive behavior disorder and intergenerational attachment patterns: a comparison of clinic-referred and normally functioning preschoolers and their mothers. *Journal of Consulting and Clinical Psychology*, 64, 357–65.

Denham, S. A. (1986). Social cognition, prosocial behavior, and emotion in preschoolers: contextual validation. *Child Development*, 57, 194–201.

Dlugokinski, E. (1984). Developing cooperative school environments for children. *Elementary School Guidance and Counselling*, 18, 209–15.

143

Doise, W. and Mugny, G. (1984). *The social development of the intellect.* Oxford: Pergamon.

Dolgin, K. G. and Kim, S. (1994). Adolescents' disclosure to best and good friends. *Social Development,* 3, 146–57.

Doll, B. (1996). Children without friends: implications for practice and policy. *School Psychology Review,* 25, 165–83.

Douvan, E. and Adelson, J. (1966). *The adolescent experience.* New York: Wiley.

DuBois, D. L. and Hirsch, B. J. (1993). School/nonschool friendship patterns in early adolescence. *Journal of Early Adolescence,* 13, 102–22.

Duck, S. W. (1975). Personality similarity and friendship choices by adolescents. *European Journal of Social Psychology,* 5, 351–65.

Dunn, J., Slomkowski, C., Donelan, N. and Herrera, C. (1995). Conflict, understanding, and relationships: developments and differences in the preschool years. *Early Education and Development,* 6, 303–16.

Dunphy, D. C. (1963). The social structure of urban adolescent peer groups. *Society,* 26, 230–46.

Dunphy, D. C. (1972). Peer group socialization. In: F. J. Hunt (ed.), *Socialization in Australia.* Sydney: Angus & Robertson.

Durkin, K. (1995). *Developmental social psychology.* Cambridge, MA: Blackwell.

Earn, B. M. and Sobol, M. P. (1990). A categorical analysis of children's attributions for social success and failure. *Psychological Record,* 40, 173–85.

Eder, D. and Hallinan, M. (1978). Sex differences in children's friendship. *American Sociological Review,* 43, 237–50.

Elbedour, S., Shulman, S. and Kedem, P. (1997). Adolescent intimacy. *Journal of Cross-Cultural Psychology,* 28, 5–22.

Elkind, D. (1967). Egocentrism in adolescence. *Child Development,* 38, 1025–34.

Elkind, D. (1978). Understanding the young adolescent. *Adolescence,* 13, 127–34.

Elovitz, G. P. and Salvia, J. (1982). Attractiveness as a biasing factor in the judgements of school psychologists. *Journal of School Psychology,* 20, 339–45.

Erikson, E. H. (1963). *Childhood and society* (2nd edn). New York: Norton.

Erwin, P. G. (1993). *Friendship and peer relations in children.* Chichester: Wiley.

Erwin, P. G. (1996). Intervention strategies and social indices of children's peer relationships. Paper presented to the International Society for the Study of Behavioural Development, Quebec, Canada, August.

Erwin, P. G. and Calev, A. (1984). Beauty: more than skin deep? *Journal of Social and Personal Relationships*, 1, 359–61.

Etaugh, C. and Liss, M. B. (1992). Home, school, and playroom: training grounds for adult gender roles. *Sex Roles*, 26, 129–47.

Fagot, B. I. (1977). Consequences of moderate cross-gender behavior in preschool children. *Child Development*, 48, 902–7.

Fagot, B. I. (1981). Continuity and change in play styles as a function of sex of child. *International Journal of Behavioral Development*, 4, 37–43.

Feiring, C. and Lewis, M. (1989). The social networks of girls and boys from early through middle childhood. In: D. Belle (ed.), *Children's social networks and social supports.* New York: Wiley.

Felson, R. B. (1985). Reflected appraisal and the development of self. *Social Psychology Quarterly*, 48, 71–8.

Feshbach, N. D. (1978). Studies of empathic behavior in children. In: B. A. Maher (ed.), *Progress in experimental personality research, vol. 8.* New York: Academic Press.

Festinger, L. (1954). A theory of social comparison processes. *Human Relations*, 7, 117–40.

Fine, G A. (1980). The natural history of preadolescent male friendship groups. In: H. C. Foot, A. J. Chapman and J. R. Smith (eds), *Friendship and social relations in children.* Chichester: Wiley.

Fine, G A. (1987). Friends, impression management, and preadolescent behavior. In: S. R. Asher and J. M. Gottman (eds), *The development of children's friendships.* Cambridge: Cambridge University Press.

Fisher, S. (1995). The amusement arcade as a social space for adolescents. *Journal of Adolescence*, 18, 71–86.

Freedman, R. J. (1984). Reflections on beauty as it relates to health in adolescent females. *Women & Health*, 9, 29–45.

Frey, C. U. and Rothlisberger, C. (1996). Social support in healthy adolescents. *Journal of Youth and Adolescence*, 25, 17–31.

Furman, W. and Buhrmester, D. (1992). Age and sex differences in perceptions of networks of personal relationships. *Child Development*, 63, 103–15.

145

Furman, W., Rahe, D. F. and Hartup, W. W. (1979). Rehabilitation of socially withdrawn preschool children through mixed-age and same-age socialization. *Child Development*, 50, 915–22.

Gavin, L. A. and Furman, W. (1996). Adolescent girls' relationships with mothers and best friends. *Child Development*, 67, 375–86.

Gewirtz, J. L. and Pelaez-Nogueras, M. (1991). The attachment metaphor and the conditioning of infant separation protests. In: J. L. Gewirtz and W. M. Kurtines (eds), *Intersections with attachment*. London: Erlbaum.

Giordano, P. C. (1995). The wider circle of friends in adolescence. *American Journal of Sociology*, 101, 661–97.

Goetz, T. E. and Dweck, C. S. (1980). Learned helplessness in social situations. *Journal of Personality and Social Psychology*, 39, 246–55.

Goldstein, A. P., Gershaw, N. J. and Sprafkin, R. P. (1985). Structured learning. In: L. L'Abate and M. A. Milan (eds), *Handbook of social skills training and research*. New York: Wiley.

Gottman, J. M. (1977). Toward a definition of social isolation in children. *Child Development*, 48, 513–17.

Gottman, J. M. (1991). Finding the roots of children's problems with other children. *Journal of Social and Personal Relationships*, 8, 441–8.

Gottman, J. M., Gonso, J. and Rasmussen, B. (1975). Social interaction, social competence and friendship in children. *Child Development*, 46, 709–18.

Gottman, J., Gonso, J. and Schuler, P. (1976). Teaching social skills to isolated children. *Journal of Abnormal Child Psychology*, 4, 179–97.

Greenberg, M. T. and Marvin, R. S. (1982). Reactions of preschool children to an adult stranger: a behavioral systems approach. *Child Development*, 53, 481–90.

Greenberg, M. T., Siegel, J. M. and Leitch, C. J. (1983). The nature and importance of attachment relationships to parents and peers during adolescence. *Journal of Youth & Adolescence*, 12, 373–86.

Gresham, F. M. and Nagle, R. J. (1980). Social skills with children: responsiveness to modeling and coaching as a function of peer orientation. *Journal of Consulting and Clinical Psychology*, 18, 718–29.

Guddykunst, W. B., Ting-Toomy, S. and Nishida, T. (eds) (1996). *Communication in personal relationships across cultures*. London: Sage.

Hallinan, M. T. (1976). Friendship patterns in open and traditional classrooms. *Sociology of Education*, 49, 254–65.

Hallinan, M. T. (1979). Structural effects on children's friendships and cliques. *Social Psychology Quarterly*, 42, 43–54.

Hallinan, M. (1980). Patterns of cliquing among youth. In: H. C. Foot, A. J. Chapman and J. R. Smith (eds), *Friendship and social relations in children*. Chichester: Wiley.

Hallinan, M. T. and Tuma, N. B. (1978). Classroom effects on change in children's friendships. *Sociology of Education*, 51, 270–82.

Hansen, D. J., Nangle, D. W. and Ellis, J. T. (1996). Reconsideration of the use of peer sociometrics for evaluating social skills training. *Behavior Modification*, 20, 281–99.

Harrison, A. O., Stewart, R. B., Myambo, K. and Teveraishe, C. (1995). Perceptions of social networks among adolescents from Zimbabwe and the United States. *Journal of Black Psychology*, 21, 382–407.

Hartup, W. W. (1983). Peer relations. In: E. M. Hetherington (ed.), *Handbook of child psychology, vol. 4: Socialization, personality, and social development*. New York: Wiley.

Hartup, W. W. (1986). On relationships and development. In: W. W. Hartup and Z. Rubin (eds), *Relationships and development*. Hillsdale, NJ: Erlbaum.

Hartup, W. W. and Stevens, N. (1997). Friendship and adaptation in the life course. *Psychological Bulletin*, 121, 355–70.

Hartup, W. W., Laursen, B., Stewart, M. I. and Eastenson, A. (1988). Conflict and friendship relations of young children. *Child Development*, 59, 1590–1600.

Harvey, J. H., Weber, A. L., Yarkin, K. L. and Stewart, B. E. (1982). An attributional approach to relationships breakdown and dissolution. In: S. W. Duck (ed.), *Personal relationships, vol. 4: Dissolving personal relationships*. London: Academic Press.

Hernandez, D. J. (1997). Child development and the social demography of childhood. *Child Development*, 68, 149–69.

Hinde, R. A., Titmus, G., Easton, D. and Tamplin, A. (1985). Incidence of friendship and behaviour toward strong associates versus nonassociates in preschoolers. *Child Development*, 56, 234–45.

Hoffman, M. L. (1987). The contribution of empathy to justice and moral judgement. In: N. Eisenberg and J. Strayer (eds), *Empathy and its development*. Cambridge: Cambridge University Press.

REFERENCES

Hoffman, M. L. (1988). Moral development. In: M. Bornstein and M. Lamb (eds), *Social, emotional and personality development. Part 3 of Developmental Psychology: an advanced textbook.* London: Erlbaum.

Howes, C., Droege, K. and Matheson, C. C. (1994). Play and communicative processes within long- and short-term friendship dyads. *Journal of Social and Personal Relationships*, 11, 401–10.

Hymel, S. and Franke, S. (1985). Children's peer relations: assessing self-perceptions. In: B. H. Schneider, K. H. Rubin and J. E. Ledingham (eds), *Children's peer relations: issues in assessment and intervention.* New York: Springer-Verlag.

Hymel, S. and Rubin, K. H. (1985). Children with peer relationship and social skills problems: conceptual, methodological, and developmental issues. *Annals of Child Development*, 2, 251–97.

Inderbitzen, H. M. (1994). Adolescent peer social competence. In: T. H. Ollendick and R. J. Prinz (eds), *Advances in Clinical Child Psychology, vol. 16.* New York: Plenum.

Isabella, R. A. and Belsky, J. (1991). Interactional synchrony and the origins of infant–mother attachment: a replication study. *Child Development*, 62, 373–84.

Jacobson, J. L. (1981). The role of inanimate objects in early peer interaction. *Child Development*, 52, 618–26.

Johnson, D. W. and Johnson, R. T. (1983). Social interdependence and perceived academic and personal support in the classroom. *Journal of Social Psychology*, 120, 77–82.

Jones, D. C. and Costin, S. E. (1995). Friendship quality during preadolescence and adolescence. *Merrill Palmer Quarterly*, 41, 517–35.

Jones, W. H., Hobbs, S. A. and Hockenbury, D. (1982). Loneliness and social skill deficits. *Journal of Personality and Social Psychology*, 42, 682–9.

Juffer, F., van Ijzendoorn, M. H. and Bakermans-Kranenburg, M. J. (1997). Intervention in transmission of insecure attachment. *Psychological Reports*, 80, 531–43.

Kahen, V., Katz, L. and Gottman, J. M. (1994). Linkages between parent–child interaction and conversations of friends. *Social Development*, 3, 238–54.

Kandel, D. B. (1978). Homophily, selection, and socialization in adolescent friendships. *American Journal of Sociology*, 84, 427–36.

Kerns, K. A. (1994). A longitudinal examination of links between mother–infant attachment and children's friendships. *Journal of Social and Personal Relationships*, 11, 379–81.

Kerns, K. A., Klepac, L. and Cole, A. K. (1996). Peer relationships and preadolescents' perceptions of security in the child–mother relationship. *Developmental Psychology*, 32, 457–66.

Kerns, K. A. and Stevens, A. C. (1996). Parent–child attachment in late adolescence. *Journal of Youth and Adolescence*, 25, 323–42.

Kirchler, E., Palmonari, A. and Pombeni, M. L. (1995). Developmental tasks and adolescents' relationships with their peers and their family. In: S. Jackson and H. Rodriguez-Tomé (eds), *Adolescence and its social worlds*. Hove: Erlbaum.

Kleck, R. E. and De Jong, W. (1983). Physical disability, physical attractiveness, and social outcomes in children's small groups. *Rehabilitation Psychology*, 28, 79–91.

Kochanska, G. (1997). Mutually responsive orientation between mothers and their young children. *Child Development*, 68, 94–112.

Krollmann, M. and Krappmann, L. (1996). Attachment and children's friendships in middle childhood. Poster paper presented at the Conference of the International Society for the Study of Behavioral Development, August, Quebec City, Canada.

Kupersmidt, J. B., Coie, J. D. and Dodge, K. A. (1990). The role of peer relationships in the development of disorder. In: S. R. Asher and J. D. Coie (eds), *Peer rejection in childhood*. Cambridge: Cambridge University Press.

Kupersmidt, J. B., DeRosier, M. E. and Patterson, C. P. (1995). Similarity as the basis for children's friendships. *Journal of Social and Personal Relationships*, 12, 439–52.

Ladd, G. W. (1983). Social networks of popular, average and rejected children in social settings. *Merrill Palmer Quarterly*, 29, 282–307.

Ladd, G. W. (1990). Having friends, keeping friends, making friends, and being liked by peers in the classroom. *Child Development*, 61, 1081–1100.

Ladd, G. W. and Golter, B. S. (1988). Parents' management of preschoolers' peer relations: is it related to children's social competence? *Developmental Psychology*, 24, 109–17.

Ladd, G. W. and Kochenderfer, B. J. (1996). Linkages between friendship and adjustment during early school transitions. In: W. M.

149

Bukowski, A. F. Newcomb and W. W. Hartup (eds), *The company they keep: friendship in childhood and adolescence*. Cambridge: Cambridge University Press.

Ladd, G. W., Kochenderfer, B. J. and Coleman, C. C. (1996). Friendship quality as a predictor of young children's early school adjustment. *Child Development*, 67, 1103–18.

Ladd, G. W. and Mars, K. T. (1986). Reliability and validity of preschoolers' perceptions of peer behavior. *Journal of Clinical Child Psychology*, 15, 16–25.

LaFreniere, P. J. (1996). Co-operation as a conditional strategy among peers: influence of social ecology and kin relations. *International Journal of Behavioral Development*, 19, 39–52.

LaFreniere, P. J. and Sroufe, L. A. (1985). Profiles of peer competence in the preschool: interrelations between measures, influence of social ecology, and relation to attachment theory. *Developmental Psychology*, 21, 56–69.

Lalonde, C. E. and Chandler, M. J. (1995). False belief understanding goes to school: on the social–emotional consequences of coming early or late to a first theory of mind. *Cognition and Emotion*, 9, 167–85.

Langlois, J. H., Ritter, J. M., Casey, R. J. and Sawin, D. B. (1995). Infant attractiveness predicts maternal behaviors and attitudes. *Developmental Psychology*, 31, 464–72.

Laursen, B. (1995). Conflict and social interaction in adolescent relationships. *Journal of Research on Adolescence*, 5, 55–70.

Lempers, J. and Clark-Lempers, D. (1993). A functional comparison of same-sex and opposite-sex friendships during adolescence. *Journal of Adolescent Research*, 8, 89–103.

Levinger, G. and Levinger, A. C. (1986). The temporal course of close relationships: some thoughts about the development of children's ties. In: W. W. Hartup and Z. Rubin (eds), *Relationships and development*. Hillsdale, NJ: Erlbaum.

Lewis, M. and Brooks-Gunn, J. (1979). *Social cognition and the acquisition of self*. New York: Plenum.

Leyva, F. A. and Furth, H. G. (1986). Compromise formation in social conflicts. *Journal of Youth and Adolescence*, 15, 441–51.

Lockheed, M. E. (1986). Reshaping the social order: the case of gender segregation. *Sex Roles*, 14, 617–28.

Main, M., Kaplan, N. and Cassidy, J. (1985). Security in infancy, childhood, and adulthood: a move to the level of representation.

Monographs of the Society for Research in Child Development, 50 (whole no. 209), 66–104.

Mand, C. L. (1974). Rediscovering the fourth 'R'. *Theory into Practice*, 13, 245–51.

Marrow, A. J. (1969). *The practical theorist: the life and work of Kurt Lewin*. New York: Basic Books.

Marsh, D. T., Serafica, F. C. and Barenboim, C. (1981). Interrelationships among perspective taking, interpersonal problem-solving, and interpersonal functioning. *Journal of Genetic Psychology*, 138, 37–48.

Martin, C. L. and Little, J. K. (1990). The relation of gender understanding to children's sex-typed preferences and gender stereotypes. *Child Development*, 61, 1427–39.

Maslow, A. H. (1954). *Motivation and personality*. New York: Harper.

Matos, M., Fonseca, V., Belo, J. and Oliveira, L. (1991). Social skills training: a skill deficit and contextualist approach. Paper presented to the Annual Conference of Counselling Psychology Section of the British Psychological Society, Birmingham, June.

Matthews, K. A., Batson, C. D., Horn, J. and Rosenman, R. H. (1981). 'Principles in his nature which interest him in the fortune of others' ... The heritability of empathic concern for others. *Journal of Personality*, 49, 237–47.

McAdams, D. P. and Losoff, M. (1984). Friendship motivation in fourth and sixth graders. *Journal of Social and Personal Relationships*, 1, 12–27.

McCall, G. J. (1982). Becoming unrelated: the management of bond dissolution. In: S. W. Duck (ed.), *Personal relationships, vol. 4: Dissolving personal relationships*. London: Academic Press.

Medrich, E. A., Rosen, J., Rubin, V. and Buckley, S. (1982). *The seriousness of growing up: a study of children's lives outside school*. Berkeley, CA: University of California Press.

Meichenbaum, D. (1986). Cognitive behavior modification. In: F. H. Kanfer and A. P. Goldstein (eds), *Helping people change: a textbook of methods* (3rd edn). New York: Pergamon.

Mendelson, M. J., Aboud, F. E. and Lanthier, R. P. (1994). Personality predictors of friendship and popularity in kindergarten. *Journal of Applied Developmental Psychology*, 15, 413–35.

Mize, J. and Ladd, G. W. (1990). Toward the development of successful social skills training for preschool children. In: S. R. Asher and J. D. Coie (eds), *Peer rejection in childhood*. New York: Cambridge University Press.

151

Montemayor, R. and Flannery, D. J. (1989). A naturalistic study of the involvement of children and adolescents with their mothers and friends: developmental differences in expressive behavior. *Journal of Adolescent Research*, 4, 3–14.

Montemayor, R. and Van Komen, R. (1985). The development of sex differences in friendship patterns and peer group structure during adolescence. *Journal of Early Adolescence*, 5, 285–94.

Moore, C. (1996). Theories of mind in infancy. *British Journal of Developmental Psychology*, 14, 19–40.

Moreland, R. L. and Levine, J. M. (1982). Socialization in small groups. *Advances in Experimental Social Psychology*, 15, 137–92.

Morris, T. L., Messer, S. C. and Gross, A. M. (1995). Enhancement of the social interaction and status of neglected children: a peer-pairing approach. *Journal of Clinical Child Psychology*, 24, 11–20.

Murphy, K. and Schneider, B. (1994). Coaching socially rejected early adolescents regarding behaviours used by peers to infer liking. *Journal of Early Adolescence*, 14, 83–95.

Murray, R. (1974). The influence of crowding on children's behaviour. In: D. Cantor and T. Lee (eds), *Psychology and the built environment*. London: Architectural Press.

Nakagawa, M., Lamb, M. E. and Miyaki, K. (1992). Antecedents and correlates of the Strange Situation behavior of Japanese infants. *Journal of Cross-Cultural Psychology*, 23, 300–10.

Neckerman, H. J. (1996). The stability of social groups in childhood and adolescence: the role of the classroom social environment. *Social Development*, 5, 131–45.

Nelson, J. and Aboud, F. E. (1985). The resolution of social conflict among friends. *Child Development*, 56, 1009–17.

Nowicki, S. and Oxenford, C. (1989). The relation of hostile nonverbal communication styles to popularity in preadolescent children. *Journal of Genetic Psychology*, 150, 39–44.

Obanawa, N. and Joh, H. (1995). The influence of toys on preschool children's social behavior. *Psychologia*, 38, 70–6.

O'Connor, R. (1972). Relative efficacy of modeling, shaping, and the combined procedures for modification of social withdrawal. *Journal of Abnormal Psychology*, 79, 327–34.

O'Donnell, L. and Stueve, A. (1983). Mothers as social agents: structuring the community activities of school aged children. In: H. Z. Lopata and J. H. Pleck (eds), *Jobs and families*. Greenwich, CT: JAI.

Ogbu, J. U. (1981). Origins of human competence: a cultural–ecological perspective. *Child Development*, 52, 413–29.

Parke, R. D. and Slaby, R. G. (1983). The development of aggression. In: E. M. Hetherington (ed.), *Handbook of child psychology, vol. 4: Socialization, personality, and social development*. New York: Wiley.

Parker, J. G. and Asher, S. R. (1987). Peer relations and later personal adjustment: are low-accepted children at risk? *Psychological Bulletin*, 102, 357–89.

Parker, J. G. and Gottman, J. M. (1989). Social and emotional development in a relational context. In: T. J. Berndt and G. W. Ladd (eds), *Peer relationships in child development*. New York: Wiley.

Paterson, J., Pryor, J. and Field, J. (1995). Adolescent attachment to parents and friends in relation to aspects of self-esteem. *Journal of Youth and Adolescence*, 24, 365–76.

Peery, J. C. (1980). Neonate and adult head movement: no and yes revisited. *Developmental Psychology*, 16, 245–50.

Peplau, L. A. and Perlman, D. (1982). Perspectives on loneliness. In: L. A. Peplau and D. Perlman (eds), *Loneliness: a sourcebook of current theory, research and therapy*. New York: Wiley.

Perkins, D. F. and Lerner, R. M. (1995). Single and multiple indicators of physical attractiveness and psychosocial behaviors among young adolescents. *Journal of Early Adolescence*, 15, 269–98.

Perner, J., Ruffman, T. and Leekham, S. R. (1994). Theory of mind is contagious: you catch it from your sibs. *Child Development*, 65, 1228–38.

Perry, M. A. and Furukawa, M. J. (1986). Modeling methods. In: F. H. Kanfer and A. P. Goldstein (eds), *Helping people change: a textbook of methods* (3rd edn). New York: Pergamon.

Pettit, G. S., Clawson, M. A., Dodge, K. A. and Bates, J. E. (1996). Stability and change in peer-rejected status: the role of child behavior, parenting, and family ecology. *Merrill Palmer Quarterly*, 42, 267–94.

Pfluger, L. W. and Zola, J. M. (1974). A room planned by children. In: G. Coates (ed.), *Alternative learning environments*. Stroudsburg, PA: Dowden, Hutchinson & Ross.

Pianta, R. C., Sroufe, L. A. and Egeland, B. (1989). Continuity and discontinuity in maternal sensitivity at 6, 24, and 48 months in a high-risk sample. *Child Development*, 60, 481–7.

Putallaz, M. (1983). Predicting children's sociometric status from their behavior. *Child Development*, 54, 1417–26.

Putallaz, M. and Gottman, J. M. (1981). An interactional model of children's entry into peer groups. *Child Development*, 52, 986–94.

Ramsey, P. G. and Lasquade, C. (1996). Preschool children's entry attempts. *Journal of Applied Developmental Psychology*, 17, 135–50.

Ray, G. E., Cohen, R. and Secrist, M. E. (1995). Best friend networks of children across settings. *Child Study Journal*, 25, 169–88.

Rholes, W. S. and Ruble, D. N. (1984). Children's understanding of dispositional characteristics of others. *Child Development*, 55, 550–60.

Rice, C., Koinis, D., Sullivan, K., Tager-Flusberg, H. and Winner, E. (1997). When 3-year-olds pass the appearance–reality test. *Developmental Psychology*, 33, 54–61.

Rice, K. G. and Mulkeen, P. (1995). Relationships with parents and peers. *Journal of Adolescent Research*, 10, 338–57.

Richardson, S. A., Goodman, N., Hastorf, A. and Dornbusch, S. (1961). Cultural uniformity in reaction to physical disabilities. *American Sociological Review*, 26, 241–7.

Richardson, S. A., Ronald, L. and Kleck, R. E. (1974). The social status of handicapped and non-handicapped boys in a camp setting. *Journal of Special Education*, 8, 143–52.

Richey, M. H. and Richey, H. W. (1980). The significance of best-friend relationships in adolescence. *Psychology in the Schools*, 17, 536–40.

Richmond, V. P. (1984). Implications of quietness: some facts and speculations. In: J. A. Daly and J. C. McCrosky (eds), *Avoiding communication*. Beverly Hills, CA: Sage.

Roopnarine, J. R. (1985). Changes in peer directed behavior following preschool experience. *Journal of Personality and Social Psychology*, 48, 740–5.

Roscoe, B., Callahan, J. E. and Peterson, K. L. (1985). Physical attractiveness as a potential contributor to child abuse. *Education*, 105, 349–53.

Rosen, W. D., Adamson, L. B. and Bakeman, R. (1992). An experimental investigation of infant social referencing: mothers' messages and gender differences. *Developmental Psychology*, 28, 1172–8.

Ross, H. S. and Salvia, S. P. (1975). Attractiveness as a biasing factor in teacher judgements. *American Journal of Mental Deficiency*, 80, 96–8.

Rotenberg, K. J. (1995). Development of children's restrictive disclosure to friends. *Journal of Genetic Psychology*, 156, 279–92.

Rotenberg, K. J. and Chase, N. (1992). Development of the reciprocity of self-disclosure. *Journal of Genetic Psychology*, 153, 75–86.

Rubin, K. H. (1985). Socially withdrawn children: an 'at risk' population? In: B. H. Schneider, K. H. Rubin and J. E. Ledingham (eds), *Children's peer relations: issues in assessment and intervention*. New York: Springer-Verlag.

Rubin, K. H. and Mills, R. (1988). The many faces of social isolation in childhood. *Journal of Consulting and Clinical Psychology*, 56, 916–24.

Sanders, K. M. and Harper, L. V. (1976). Free play fantasy behavior in preschool children: relations among gender, age, season, and location. *Child Development*, 47, 1182–5.

Schaffer, H. R. (1996). *Social development*. Oxford: Blackwell.

Schneider, B. H. (1992). Didactic methods for enhancing children's peer relations: a quantitative review. *Clinical Psychology Review*, 12, 363–82.

Schultz, N. R. and Moore, D. (1989). Further reflections on loneliness research. In: M. Hojat and R. Crandall (eds), *Loneliness: theory research and applications*. Newbury Park, CA: Sage.

Schunk, D. H. (1987). Peer models and children's behavioral change. *Review of Educational Research*, 57, 149–74.

Sebald, H. and White, B. H. (1980). Teenager's divided reference groups: uneven alignment with parents and peers. *Adolescence*, 15, 980–4.

Seifer, R., Schiller, M., Sameroff, A. J. and Resnick, S. (1996). Attachment, maternal sensitivity, and infant temperament during the first year of life. *Developmental Psychology*, 32, 12–25.

Selman, R. L. (1980). *The growth of interpersonal understanding*. New York: Academic Press.

Serbin, L. A., Tonick, I. J. and Sternglanz, S. H. (1977). Shaping cooperative cross-sex play. *Child Development*, 48, 924–9.

Shantz, C. U. (1975). The development of social cognition. In: E. M. Heatherington (ed.), *Review of Child Development Research*, vol. 5. Chicago: University of Chicago Press.

Shantz, C. U. (1993). Children's conflicts: representations and lessons learned. In: R. R. Cocking and K. A. Renninger (eds), *The development and meaning of psychological distance*. Hillsdale, NJ: Erlbaum.

Shantz, D. W. (1986). Conflict, aggression and peer status: an observational study. *Child Development*, 57, 1322–32.

Shaver, P. and Hazan, C. (1989). Being lonely, falling in love: perspectives from attachment theory. In: M. Hojat and R. Crandall (eds), *Loneliness: theory, research, and applications*. Newbury Park, CA: Sage.

Shea, J. (1981). Changes in interpersonal distances and categories of play behavior in the early weeks of preschool. *Developmental Psychology*, 17, 417–25.

Shulman, S., Elicker, J. and Sroufe, L. A. (1994). Stages in friendship growth in preadolescence as related to attachment. *Journal of Social and Personal Relationships*, 11, 341–61.

Shultz, N. R. and Moore, D. (1989). Further reflections on loneliness research. In: M. Hojat and R. Crandall (eds), *Loneliness: theory, research, and applications*. Newbury Park, CA: Sage.

Shure, M. B. (1993). I can problem solve (ICPS): interpersonal cognitive problem solving for young children. *Early Child Development and Care*, 96, 49–64.

Sigman, M., Arbelle, S. and Dissanayake, C. (1995). Current research findings on childhood autism. *Canadian Journal of Psychiatry*, 40, 289–94.

Silbereisen, R. K., Noack, P. and von Eye, A. (1992). Adolescents' development of romantic friendship and change in favorite leisure contexts. *Journal of Adolescent Research*, 7, 80–93.

Siner, J. (1993). Social competence and co-operative learning. *Educational Psychology in Practice*, 9, 170–80.

Slomkowski, C. and Dunn, J. (1996). Young children's understanding of other people's beliefs and feelings and their connected communication with friends. *Developmental Psychology*, 32, 442–7.

Smetana, J. G. and Asquith, P. (1994). Adolescents' and parents' conceptions of parental authority and personal autonomy. *Child Development*, 65, 1147–62.

Smith, A. B. and Inder, P. M. (1990). The relationship of classroom organisation to cross-age and cross-sex friendships. *Educational Psychology*, 10, 127–40.

Smith, A. B. and Inder, P. M. (1993). Social interaction in same and cross gender pre-school peer groups: a participant observation study. *Educational Psychology*, 13, 29–42.

Snyder, J., West, L., Stockemer, V. and Gibbons, S. (1996). A social learning model of peer choice in the natural environment. *Journal of Applied Developmental Psychology*, 17, 215–37.

Spence, S. H. (1987). The relationship between social-cognitive skills and peer sociometric status. *British Journal of Developmental Psychology*, 5, 347–56.

Spivack, G. and Shure, M. B. (1989). Interpersonal Cognitive Problem Solving (ICPS): a competence-building primary prevention program. *Prevention in Human Services*, 6, 151–78.

Sroufe, L. A. (1979). The coherence of individual development. *American Psychologist*, 34, 834–41.

Sroufe, L. A. (1983). Infant–caregiver attachment and patterns of adaptation in preschool: the roots of maladaptation and competence. In: M. Perlmutter (ed.), *Minnesota Symposium on Child Psychology, vol. 16*. Hillsdale, NJ: Erlbaum.

Sroufe, L. A. and Fleeson, J. (1986). Attachment and the construction of relationships. In: W. W. Hartup and Z. Rubin (eds), *Relationships and development*. Hillsdale, NJ: Erlbaum.

Sroufe, L. A. and Jacobvitz, D. (1989). Diverging pathways, developmental transformations, multiple etiologies and the problem of continuity in development. *Human Development*, 32, 196–203.

Stewart, S. L. and Rubin, K. H. (1995). The social problem-solving skills of anxious-withdrawn children. *Development and Psychopathology*, 7, 323–36.

Sullivan, H. S. (1953). *The interpersonal theory of psychiatry*. New York: Norton.

Tan, D. T. and Singh, R. (1995). Attitudes and attraction: a developmental study of the similarity–attraction and dissimilarity–repulsion hypotheses. *Personality and Social Psychology Bulletin*, 21, 975–86.

Thorne, B. (1986). Girls and boys together . . . but mostly apart: gender arrangements in elementary schools. In: W. W. Hartup and Z. Rubin (eds), *Relationships and development*. Hillsdale, NJ: Erlbaum.

Toner, M. A. and Munro, D. (1996). Peer-social attributions and self-efficacy of peer-rejected preadolescents. *Merrill Palmer Quarterly*, 42, 339–57.

Troy, M. and Sroufe, L. A. (1987). Victimization among preschoolers: role of attachment relationship history. *Journal of the Academy of Child & Adolescent Psychiatry*, 26, 166–72.

Urberg, K. A., Degirmencioglu, S. M., Tolson, J. M. and Halliday-Scher, K. (1995). The structure of adolescent peer networks. *Developmental Psychology*, 31, 540–7.

Van Vliet, W. (1981). The environmental context of children's friendships: an empirical and conceptual examination of the role of child density. *EDRA: Environmental Design Research Association*, 12, 216–24.

Vandell, D. L. and Wilson, K. S. (1987). Infants' interactions with mother, sibling, and peer: contrasts and relationships between interaction systems. *Child Development*, 58, 176–86.

Vandell, D. L., Wilson, K. S. and Buchanan, N. R. (1980). Peer interaction in the first year of life: an examination of its structure, content and sensitivity. *Child Development*, 51, 481–8.

Vargo, B. (1995) Are withdrawn children at risk? *Canadian Journal of School Psychology*, 11, 166–77.

Venberg, E. M., Ewell, K. K., Beery, S. H. and Abwender, D. A. (1994). Sophistication of adolescents' interpersonal negotiation strategies and friendship formation after relocation. *Journal of Research on Adolescence*, 4, 5–19.

Waas, G. A. and Honer, S. A. (1990). Situational attributions and dispositional inferences: the development of peer reputation. *Merrill Palmer Quarterly*, 36, 2, 239–60.

Waldrop, M. F. and Halverson, C. F. (1975). Intensive and extensive peer behavior: longitudinal and cross-sectional analyses. *Child Development*, 46, 19–26.

Wasserstein, S. B. and La Greca, A. M. (1996). Can peer support buffer against behavioral consequences of parental discord? *Journal of Clinical Child Psychology*, 25, 177–82.

Weiss, R. S. (1989). Reflections on the present state of loneliness research. In: M. Hojat and R. Crandall (eds), *Loneliness: theory, research, and applications*. Newbury Park, CA: Sage.

Wellman, H. M. and Banerjee, M. (1991). Mind and emotion. *British Journal of Developmental Psychology*, 9, 191–214.

Wentzel, K. R. and Asher, S. R. (1995). The academic lives of neglected, rejected, popular, and controversial children. *Child Development*, 66, 754–63.

Werebe, M. (1987). Friendship and dating relationships among French adolescents. *Journal of Adolescence*, 10, 269–89.

Whiting, B. B. and Edwards, C. P. (1988). *Children of different worlds*. Cambridge, MA: Harvard University Press.

Youngblade, L. M. and Belsky, J. (1989). Child maladjustment, infant–parent attachment security and dysfunctional peer relationships in toddlerhood. *Topics in Early Childhood Special Education*, 9, 1–15.

Youngblade, L. M. and Belsky, J. (1992). Parent–child antecedents of 5-year-olds' close friendships: a longitudinal analysis. *Developmental Psychology*, 28, 700–13.

Youniss, J. and Volpe, J. (1978). A relational analysis of children's friendships. In: W. Damon (ed.), *New directions for child development*, vol. 1. San Francisco, CA: Jossey-Bass.

Zahn, G. L., Kagan, S. and Widaman, K. F. (1986). Cooperative learning and classroom climate. *Journal of School Psychology*, 24, 351–62.

Zajonc, R. B. (1968). Attitudinal effects of mere exposure. *Journal of Personality and Social Psychology Monograph Supplement*, 9, 1–27.

Zakin, D. F., Blyth, D. A. and Simmons, R. G. (1984). Physical attractiveness as a mediator of the impact of early pubertal changes in girls. *Journal of Youth and Adolescence*, 13, 439–50.

Zimbardo, P. G. (1977). *Shyness: what it is, what to do about it*. New York: Jove.

Zimbardo, P. G. and Radl, S. L. (1981). *The shy child*. New York: McGraw-Hill.

Zisman, P. and Wilson, V. (1992). Table hopping in the cafeteria. *Anthropology and Education Quarterly*, 23, 199–220.

Index

intimacy 11; in adolescence
72–3; *see also* social
support

loneliness 6, 15, 109–10;
frequency 110
loneliness and intimacy 110
loneliness and patterns of self-
disclosure 110

Maslow, A. H. 5
modelling 125–6

neighbourhood, physical
environment 92–4
nurturance *see* social support

obligations of friendship 11
open classroom 99–101

parenting styles 22–3, 91
peer contact as therapy 130–2
peer groups 65–6; activity
78
peer groups entry, difficulties
113; *see also* conformity
peer interaction, developmental
patterns 59–62
peer relationships and cognitive
development 7–8
physical appearance 10
physical handicap 105–7; social
consequences 107; *see also*
physical appearance
popularity 57–8; *see also* peer
groups
poverty *see* social class
precipitating factors in
relationship problems
112–13
preventing relationship
difficulties 15
proximity 10, 100; functional
92–3

reciprocity in relationship
48–9
reducing sex segregation 66
reference group 73
relationship collapse 12–13;
see also relationship
stages
relationship problems 15, 111;
see also loneliness;
shyness
relationship problems and
supportive relationships
113–14
relationship problems,
implications for later
adjustment 115–16
relationship stages 9–12
relationships with parents 73
role-taking 38, 42–5

school organisation and sex
segregation 99
Self 38; development of 39–40
self-consciousness and role-
taking ability 45; *see also*
Selman, R. L.
self-disclosure 11
Selman, R. L. 43–5
sex segregation in relationships
14–15, 83
shaping 124–5
shyness 15, 107–9
shyness, in adolescence 109
shyness, effects of 108
similarity-attraction 7, 11; in
adolescence 75–7;
see also consensual
validation
social class 91–2
social cognition, defined 38
social cognitive development 14,
38
social cognitive processes 14, 38;
see also attribution